RELIGIOUS BELIEFS

OF

AMERICAN SCIENTISTS

RELIGIOUS
BELIEFS
OF
AMERICAN
SCIENTISTS

Edward LeRoy Long, Jr.

GREENWOOD PRESS, PUBLISHERS
WESTPORT, CONNECTICUT

To Dot

without whose help this book would never have made its deadlines, and without whose love its completion would have little meaning.

PREFACE

THIS is a book about other men's books; it therefore attempts to convey other men's thoughts as well as to relate them to some over-all pattern. Its purpose, justification, and structure are explained in the introductory chapter; this preface merely sends it on its way.

No one can foresee how a manuscript will fare in print, and what is more, will ever measure the full dimension of its impact. It is thus a sober moment during which an author writes a preface — which for him is both retrospect and anticipation. Books must be sent forth on faith — this one is no exception to the rule. Its overt aim is not to convert, but to inform; not to argue a case, but to report a history. Nevertheless, it is sent forth with a prayer that it will witness to the truth of God in Christ.

The many who have helped in the preparation of this volume know who they are. Public mention in printed words would do nothing to increase my warmly felt appreciation for their aid. In a project like the writing of a book one discovers a community in Christ that searches for the truth about him and becomes debtor to all whose yen for knowledge is finally a thirst for faith.

E. L. L., Jr.

Longview
Canaan, New York
Summer, 1951

CONTENTS

INTRODUCTION

" It would not be difficult to come to an agreement as to what we understand by science. Science is the century-old endeavor to bring together by means of systematic thought the perceptible phenomena of this world into as thoroughgoing an association as possible. To put it boldly, it is the attempt at the posterior reconstruction of existence by the process of conceptualization. But when asking myself what religion is, I cannot think of the answer so easily. And even after finding an answer which may satisfy me at the particular moment, I still remain convinced that I can never under any circumstances bring together, even to a slight extent, all those who have given the question serious considera-tion." [1] — Albert Einstein.

STATEMENTS by natural scientists about matters religious have never failed to attract public attention. It might even be suggested that personal credos of men like Albert Einstein and Robert Millikan are as popularly known as the theological writings of men like Karl Barth and Reinhold Niebuhr. That the credos of scientists have affected the crosscurrents of thought in modern life needs no detailed elaboration. Eddington, Jeans, Du Noüy, Mather — these are well-known names in academic life and household names in many less sophisticated circles. As for the impact of these men upon religious thought, the not uncommon pulpit practice of regarding them as authoritative religious thinkers is sufficient evidence of their influence.

Special public interest in the credos of scientists is perhaps explained by the contemporary prestige of things scientific. Out of this grows a feeling that since truth about the natural order comes from the scientific scholar so also should truth about the religious order. This is based upon a *non sequitur* and is one of the ensnaring delusions of our age. Or, perhaps the credos of natural scientists attract interest because there is still a sufficient residue of the science-religion controversy abroad to insure that for some at least the very fact that a scientist should concern himself with matters religious is itself an oddity. This is based upon a prejudice and reflects an attitude toward the relation of science and religion that is still living in the past. Public enthusiasm for either reason is not scholarly interest.

This book is a study of the religious credos written by natural scientists. It is a critical survey of writings too often regarded uncritically. It is an attempt to look systematically at the religious writings of scientists and to answer questions such as the following: What do scientists as a group have to say about the meaning of life? Does what they say relate itself to the wider sweep of philosophical and religious thought? Is the religion of scientists characterized by any uniqueness? On what grounds do scientists base their religious faith? Do scientists follow either a consistent or a uniform pattern in dealing with the relationship of science to religion?

What constitutes a scientist's credo? Not only what he has to say about God or his existence. Not only what he has to say about man or the ethical principles by which he should guide his conduct. But rather the way in which a scientist interprets the meaning of life and expresses his expectations for it. A credo is a philosophy of life, a guiding rule of conduct, a personal testimony, a basic outlook toward existence.

In the material below there are credos of many different sorts. Some are written by men of Jewish, Roman, and Protestant persuasion; others by men of no traditional persuasion or individuals who oppose religion. Protestant liberals and strong fundamentalists are both represented. Men who find science and invention truly great boons to man and those who suggest the enduring values of life to be other than material offer their contrasting views. It is precisely this spread of thought that attracts our attention, and no arbitrary definition of religiosity should be allowed to delineate the field of inquiry.

But lest the material grow unwieldy and reap chaos instead of insight, defining boundaries are observed. This work considers the thought of scientists who have written book-length credos. A book may contain no more, even less, genuine contribution to human insight than a speech or a magazine article. But a book is presumptive evidence that a man has taken his speculations with sufficient earnestness to set them down in a unified, and usually coherent, form; that he regards them with sufficient care to note them for the stable record and run the risk of their preservation for posterity.

Then, too, our attention is confined to a specific group of scientists, the natural scientists. Religion is not a part of the subject matter of their professional concern. This emphasizes that this is not a study of how science is related to religion; it is a story of how scientists who concern themselves with the study of nature look at the meaning of life.

The distinction made in German between the natural sciences, *Naturwissenschaften,* and the sciences of man, *Geisteswissenschaften,* is of help here. The relationship between natural science and religion has achieved a certain stability by now — perhaps no better than a truce — which is not to be found between the human sciences and religion. There was a time when natural science and religion were at loggerheads, and thus in all the writings there is evidenced a continual concern to show a basis for the reconciliation of science and religion. In some of the credos old antagonisms still appear, but at least the lines of battle are defined and the alternative solutions evident. What is thus clarified in the case of the older sciences is still a problem with the younger ones like sociology, psychology, and anthropology.

We are going to look at twentieth century Americans. This will confine attention to a group of men with a similar cultural background. This background includes the advance and consolidation of large-scale science. There are many significant reactions on the part of the scientists to this phenomenal growth of technology; these reactions often aid in understanding the religious outlook of a particular individual. By picking a group of twentieth century Americans we find men having at their disposal historical knowledge of the great struggle of Galileo against scholastic Aristotelianism backed by Church authority. This controversy accounts for tacit assumptions in much of the thought. Not only does it warn of the possible arrogance of ecclesiastical power, thereby subtly placing religion in a defensive role; but its aftermath provides a possible prototype for the mutual tolerance of scientific activity and religious faith. Again, the fifty years chosen include scientists in the midst of another controversy, not unlike the older one. The struggle over evolution reached its height in America in the mid-twenties, and our study provides ample opportunity to observe how scientists themselves act in a controversy of this character.

A word of caution: This is not a systematic treatment of the relationship of science to culture. We are interested in personal credos, not in sweeping trends. Concretely, we are not interested so much in the struggle of religious literalism against the teaching of evolution as evidenced in the Scopes trial as in how individual scientists felt both about the trial and about the issues involved in the struggle out of which it grew.

A study of the religion of scientists was undertaken some years ago by Cyprian L. Drawbridge.[2] He sent questionnaires to members of the Royal Society, seeking to ascertain the number of scientists who believed in God. He came to the quantitative conclusion that the percentage of scientists within this rough measure of religious faith was about the same as that in the population in general. While Drawbridge dealt mainly with the British scene, the American scene was analyzed in studies by Harvey C. Lehman and Paul A. Witty.[3] These men analyzed the " distinguished " scientists in *Who's Who in America* and found that 25.4 per cent reported themselves as church members. This compared closely to the general population. In both these studies, however, questions as to the particular type of religious outlook these scientists held were ignored.

It is the questions these studies ignored that concern us. No answer to the question as to how many scientists are religious is given in this book. This requires methodology belonging elsewhere than in the philosophy of religion. The proper questions for us are: How many different types of religious philosophy are found among natural scientists? Why are these beliefs attractive to the scientists? What are the philosophical categories that appeal to scientists as they view life and religion?

The definition of a scientist as used in this book has already been limited by the term " natural " and thus includes mostly physicists, chemists, biologists, geologists, zoologists, engineers, and botanists. Since medical doctors are particularly prone to express their views on religious matters, we have included them; theirs is a status with respect to science somewhat like that of engineers. Both apply and use the results of science in social and humanitarian situations.

What measure of scientific competence has been employed to select the men studied here? Many of the men discussed are without equals in their respective fields. But ours is not the right to discuss great names alone, and so we include in the discussion all those men who have written credos and who fit the following quite loose criteria of being scientists: (1) holding a chair in an academic institution in the field of science or a research position in industry; (2) being listed in *American Men of Science.* Where possible both standards are used, the attempt throughout being to avoid an overstringency that would rule out the pluralistic element and an overlaxity that would include quacks whose scientific status is without justification or foundation.

The following is not a hit-and-miss collection of bright ideas. This can be seen in one instance by observing the logical unity of the material. Most of the live options for a philosophy of life are discussed. The search for these credos started with the reading of the obvious material, the works of Millikan, Compton, and Du Noüy. It continued with a scanning of library stacks, book by book, within the pertinent classifications, for the unknown credos of significance for the study. From these two sources, footnotes and cross references led to still more works. In due season these turned up books already read rather than new material, and at this point — interestingly enough the point at which the logical pattern completed itself — the feeling was inescapable that here was a significant body of material. Finally, all the works of individual men thus discovered were read, to do full justice to each man on the basis of his total available writings.

Not every individual discovered in this process has been presented. A few have been left out, either because they duplicate a position better represented by other men or because their thought is not sufficiently developed to form a unified outlook. No doubt certain men of peripheral interest have not come to the writer's attention; it would be presumptuous to suppose that one had made the final study or the exhaustive search.

In this presentation our concern is with the gist, the essential attempt, and not the minute details of each man's thought. To concern ourselves with the details would be to bog down in peripheral issues. It would also be to shift the nature of this writing from a study to a supposed source book. This work is not a substitute for the reading of the originals, but rather a guide to the contents of the originals that those who wish may turn quickly to such areas of concern as interest them.

We have avoided reducing the thought of these scientists to technical philosophical categories. Sometimes their thought fits into such categories without forcing or alteration, but at other times the scientists are so uniquely individualistic that no such pigeonholing will capture their thought honestly. To be sure, another man's thought can never be treated without recourse to certain categories of exposition. But technical categories are sometimes less helpful than homespun ones. In the following treatment, therefore, we have tried to find a mode of expressing the scientists' thought that does justice to their individuality and at the same time relates their thought to larger patterns. In this way the contributions and suggestions met in the credos of the scientists can be approached on their own terms, perhaps even captured with their own flavor, and still have significance for those who use more standard philosophical jargon.

Perhaps in this way the hope of Dr. Arthur Compton can be realized when he suggests:

"It is in much the same spirit [the recognition that truth is arrived at through a series of successive approximations], it seems to me, that the scientist must venture into such related fields as philosophy and religion. He knows he will probably make false steps. Yet unless he brings before the educated public those findings which appear to him significant, the philosopher and theologian have no means of learning of those findings. If the scientist's amateur interpretations are found faulty, these faults and inadequacies can be remedied by those having a more extensive philosophical background." [4]

And so we turn to the scientists themselves: first, to those whose essential approach is to start with what science has to say about the world in which man lives and move from this to a religious credo; secondly, to men who start with an accepted religious outlook and seek to reconcile it with, or support it by reference to, scientific considerations.

A brief word to restate what has already been implied. The quotation from Dr. Einstein that heads this chapter clearly suggests it. The definition of " science " is comparatively easy, and when one speaks of " science " there is general agreement as to what one means. The definition of " religion " is impossible without due allowance for wide variation. Scientists have no uniform attitude toward religion but many attitudes, each of which requires appreciation for its own terms and its own way of dealing with the fundamental questions of life.

PART ONE

APPROACHES THROUGH SCIENCE

I

GOD AS COSMIC STRUCTURE

" The traits often assigned to Deity, the qualities of personality, of love, of wrath, properly belong only to poetry and symbolism. Even in imagination we cannot expand any human trait to Infinity. To understand the Infinite, one must wait, as it were, on His level . . ." [1] — David Starr Jordan.

THE religious idea of God and the scientific idea of an orderly cosmos have never been completely alien to each other. It is not surprising, therefore, to find the religious outlook of certain scientists characterized by an identity between the order of nature and the religious idea of God. They view God as a cosmic principle, or, more exactly perhaps, a cosmic principle as God. For them, the orderliness of the universe carries religious meaning; God is equated with cosmic structure.

This type of religious philosophy is found in Albert Einstein's " cosmic religion." For Einstein there is genuine inspiration in the contemplation of an orderly cosmos:

" The cosmic religious experience is the strongest and noblest driving force behind scientific research. . . . What a deep faith in the rationality of the structure of the world and what a longing to understand even a small glimpse of the reason revealed in the world there must have been in Kepler and Newton to enable them to unravel the mechanism of the heavens, in long years of lonely work! " [2]

For Einstein, religious knowledge is always a limited rational comprehension. He speaks of knowing "that what is impenetrable to us really exists," of trying "humbly to comprehend even an infinitesimal part of the intelligence manifested in nature." [3] He asks, "How can [the human mind] conceive of a God before whom a thousand years and a thousand dimensions are as one? " [4]

This mood is neither a defense nor a criticism of the role of reason in religious thought. It is a sort of intellectual mysticism which says at one place, "The path to genuine religiosity does not lie through . . . blind faith, but through striving after rational knowledge," [5] and at another, "The most beautiful thing we can express is the mysterious." [6] It is an awareness of the "nobility and marvelous" order in the cosmos which in its grandeur overwhelms the individual.

One applies the term "mysticism" to Einstein only with careful qualification. His is not a religious mysticism signifying a flight into fantasy. It is, as Philipp Frank points out, related to "hard facts." [7] It is based upon the idea of a cosmic intelligence comprehended by human intelligence. It seeks no mystical bliss as an escape from the realities of experience. And yet it is mysticism. Einstein feels a sense of awe before the simplicity and beauty of the cosmic structure as expressed in mathematical form. This awe comes, not simply from our ability to understand the mathematical structure, but in response to our inability to understand finally its utter simplicity. This awe is a response to something we cannot fully comprehend, and yet we know it exists. In this "not knowing about knowing" we may see an idea to which the religious term "mysticism" is not inappropriate, especially since Einstein himself uses the term in pointing to the religious and reverent aspect involved in it.

In justifying his faith, Einstein sketches and criticizes what he regards as alternative levels of religious understanding.

In his book *Cosmic Religion,* he treats the first level as primitive religion — a religion of fear, seeking the appeasement of its deity. This religion is stabilized (though not caused) by the work of a priestly cast. On the second level are the religions that spring from social feelings. On this level the idea of God includes moral considerations. Social religion thinks of a God who rewards or punishes men, who comforts and sustains them as individuals, who is conceived in the likeness of man. The third level, found only in gifted individuals, and seldom in its pure form, involves a feeling of " the vanity of human desires and aims, and the nobility and marvelous order which are revealed in nature and the world of thought." [8] This " cosmic religious sense " is particularly to be noted in Buddhism; it cannot be the basis of a Church whose doctrine embodies it; it may be the possession of heretics.

It is on this third and highly abstract and sophisticated level that we must understand Einstein's idea of God. Einstein would jealously preserve the cosmic religious sense from all anthropomorphism in understanding God. He distrusts theologies, creeds, and traditional religious categories, since these employ anthropomorphic terms and thus limit God to manlike categories. Einstein's terms for God include " infinite," " impenetrable," " rational cosmic intelligence," but not " Almighty," " self-revealing One," or " Lord of history." God is identified with a complete and orderly rational structure; he is not a purposing will governing nature. As Einstein says, " The idea of a Being who interferes with the sequence of events in the world is absolutely impossible." [9]

Einstein's idea of God is based upon a view of the rational character of reality. The concept of orderly cosmic structure plays a major role in this view. Man's mind meets the rational substructure of all reality, however partially. The experience of knowing, involving the mystical awe noted above, becomes the experience of God. God is found in the "knowability" of the world; this "knowability" is the cosmic substructure of reality.

Einstein is anxious to avoid anthropomorphism. There is reason to doubt that he succeeds. The order that he attributes to God does not necessarily have an ontological reality. It may be no more than a mode of man's looking at the world of nature. This problem has been raised by the conventionalist schools of the philosophy of science. They hold that the so-called "laws" of nature are convenient, and even arbitrary, configurations imposed upon an external environment by the mind of man. If this is so, we hardly can find in the order seen by science an escape from anthropomorphism. Even if the content of human knowledge is viewed as but a dim reflection of the order beyond, how can we be certain that the reflection is not seen from the surface of a man-made whirlpool?

Then, too, in seeking to get away from anthropomorphism, Einstein falls into a worse alternative. He makes God subhuman, since he is driven to say that God cannot concern himself with realms of being other than law and order. The realms of history, of personality, of value — these lie outside the nature of God. God does not embody purpose; he can have no outpouring love for man.

How, then, in his religious philosophy as a whole, does Einstein make a place for purpose — for morality and the historical drives of man? He embraces humanism, placing the moral aspect of religion directly upon the shoulders of man. Whereas God is impersonal, the cultural manifestation of religion depends upon the cultivation of the good life by individuals.

"Both churches and universities — insofar as they live up to their true function — serve the ennoblement of the individual." [10]

"In their struggle for the ethical good, teachers of religion must have the stature to give up the doctrine of a personal God, that is, give up that source of fear and hope which in the past placed such vast power in the hands of priests. In their labors they will have to avail themselves of those forces which are capable of cultivating the Good, the True, and the Beautiful in humanity itself." [11]

But here there is an interesting vacillation between two emphases in Einstein's thought. On the one hand he suggests that "it is a hopeless undertaking to debate about fundamental value judgments," [12] that "for pure logic all axioms are arbitrary, including the axioms of ethics," while on the other hand he suggests that "ethical directives can be made rational and coherent by logical thinking and empirical knowledge." [13] Which way is it to be? Is there the possibility of a humanistic religion, or is all concern for such matters purely an individual affair? Are skeptical positivists to claim Einstein, or is the Society for Ethical Culture to find in him a firm supporter? In the main Einstein's attitude tends to fit the concern of the latter group. He makes an analogy between ethics and mathematics. Each involves arbitrary presuppositions, but each is dependent upon the test of experience for a working vindication of the axioms. Certain axioms emerge as true and normative for the guidance of man; these _ome ethical standards.

Einstein is an ethical idealist, quick to champion socially liberal causes and often optimistic in his expectation for society as a whole. He writes as follows:

"I am firmly convinced that the passionate will for justice and truth has done more to improve man's condition than calculating political shrewdness which in the long run only breeds general distrust. Who can doubt that Moses was a better leader of humanity than Machiavelli?" [14]

Out of this idealism Einstein's specific political opinions quite naturally spring. These include pacifism, modified only for the case of Nazi tyranny; his democratic socialism, without Marxist emphasis upon the class struggle; his Zionism, more cultural than political in its basic feeling; and his strong advocacy of world government, for which he feels nations should be willing to limit their sovereignty. These ethical positions witness to Einstein's strong and driving humanitarian concern and his role as a citizen vitally interested in the affairs of the world.

To use Einstein's religious ideas as illustrative of a basic type of religious outlook may be to eclipse the full richness of his thought. Einstein writes a great deal of nontechnical material, and his works in this area are well known. There is no substitute in understanding the inner compulsions of Einstein's religious attitude for reading his original works. This is true, even though his contribution to religion is not commensurate with his contribution to scientific theory. He deals quickly with such issues as he raises and is more concerned to express his sense of awe and wonder before the orderly structure of the cosmos than to deal in a full and critical fashion with the philosophical matters that he touches. Thus, while Einstein gives popular and succinct expression to a recurrent idea of God, his thought does not push back a frontier. Einstein has not superseded Spinoza.

A cosmic religion similar to that of Einstein is threaded through the writings of David Starr Jordan, an ichthyologist and onetime chancellor of Stanford University. The quotation at the beginning of this chapter is representative of Jordan's thought, reflecting as it does his distrust of anthropomorphism. A quotation from another source in which Jordan speaks of the " God of things that are " discloses a similar sentiment:

" The infinite expanse of the universe, its growth through

immeasurable periods of time, the boundless range of its changes, and the rational order that pervades it all, seem to demand an infinite intelligence behind its manifestations. This intelligence we cannot define but of this we feel sure, it can be no mere tribal god, nor one busy with schemes and plans man-fashion and thwarted by his own creations." [15]

In Jordan the " all-pervading order in the universe seems to imply . . . a majestic, indefinable entity which in our limited vocabulary we may designate as Supreme Intelligence." [16] Here a rational structure is assigned the place of God. It is a rational structure, not fully comprehendible in human terms, that " envelops or constitutes the universe." Jordan supports his contention that we cannot fully know God by suggesting we cannot fully know many scientific facts. For example, we do not know all the details regarding crystal formation. This, however, is no grounds for nonbelief, for we can no more certainly conceive of God's nonexistence than we can know all the details of his nature.

Unlike Einstein, however, Jordan finds a relationship between his metaphysics and his morality. He suggests that "two elements, rational order and love," emanate from the same source. [17] Thus when man loves, he acts creatively and in keeping with the essential nature of the universe. In the universe God is truth, while within God is love. [18]

A careful delineation of Jordan's thought at this point will prevent a misunderstanding. Jordan is not undercutting his view of God as an orderly structure by attributing a personal quality to God; he is extending his concept of God's structure to include love as a principle. Love in God is not will and volition, but an inexorable moral reality over man, even as the cosmic structure is an ontological reality over nature. Love in this sense is goodness to those who live harmoniously with it, severity to those who flout its dictates.

The belief in God as cosmic principle may present little if any opportunity for the religious feeling of personal relationship with God. God is a law that helps those who obey it and breaks those who flout it. God is perfection and order whose form and essence are unchanged and even unconcerned with the historical destiny of men. Hermann Weyl, himself a mathematician rather than a natural scientist, has suggested this as a strength rather than a weakness in a cosmic idea of God. For Weyl history and morals evidence suffering and evil in the world while our knowledge of physical order gives us " a vision of the flawless harmony which is in conformity with sublime reason." [19]

An interesting variation of the idea of God as a cosmic principle has been made by Arvid Reuterdahl, a former president of the Ramsey Institute of Technology. Reuterdahl's thought is difficult to relate to the main-stream patterns of philosophical discourse. He thinks in terms of a self-styled scheme and a unique vocabulary that is typically illustrated by: soul is mind-energy, or cosmoenergy in the bodily garment of conscious matter. Reuterdahl's book *The God of Science* [20] resembles a religious tract. Many lines, even whole paragraphs, are capitalized for emphasis, and the type itself is large and bold. Despite this fact, however, Reuterdahl's thought deserves a hearing. Reuterdahl is not without his standing as a scientist, having held professorships in either physics or engineering at such places as Colby College, the Polytechnic Institute of Kansas, and the College of St. Thomas, and being a fellow of the American Association of the Advancement of Science and other recognized brotherhoods of scientific workers.

Reuterdahl is carried away with his own scheme. This is evidenced indirectly by his failure to deal with his subject in normal philosophical categories and more directly by his own boasting claim:

"I have developed a new science, to which I have given the name 'Scientific Theism.' . . . [It] is the first system in which such subjects as 'God,' 'Soul,' 'Immortality,' etc., are treated from the strictly scientific standpoint." [21]

In this claim Reuterdahl throws aside cosmic mysticism — he does not wish to wait on the impenetrable, but rather claims to manage it within his own categories. The qualification of man's capacity to know the existence of the infinite found in Einstein is banished here by a rational scheme of a most blatant sort:

"Action at one Material Point + Aether + the Intangible X = Action at some other Material Point

Movement in one Atom + the Intangible X = the Opposite Movement in another Atom or Atoms

Change of Energy at one point + the Intangible X = An Opposite Change of energy at some other point or points

Physical Action, explained in terms of Scientific Concepts + the Intangible X = Opposite Physical Action in terms of appropriate Scientific Concepts." [22]

"Since *God is this Intangible X,*" Reuterdahl argues, "it follows that true Science requires the Existence of God as a fact. Hence the term *Scientific Theism* is vindicated, and the Existence of God has been proved from scientific facts." [23]

Reuterdahl's confusion of words sheds little clear light on whether this Intangible X is really a first cause (a reality prior to nature) or a cosmic structure (the reality of nature itself). We are treating him as a limited case of belief in cosmic structure because three points he makes elsewhere in his work tend to throw his thought on this side of the argument. He says at one place that Scientific Theism disagrees with all solipsism and all anthropomorphism of the man-God

Myth.[24] This carries through the theme of other representatives of cosmic religion that God is not understood in anthropomorphic terms. At another place Reuterdahl points out that " an Absolute is a Permanent and Unchanging Relationship " and that God is " *The Totality of the Absolutes,* the Soul of Deific Energy." [25] Reduced to manageable philosophical categories, this is a God of structure. A third reference, akin to the second, involves Reuterdahl's conception of a hierarchy of being, including seven levels.

" 1. Space is the Body of Time
" 2. Physical Matter is the Body of Physical Energy
" 3. Living Matter is the Body of Vital Energy
" 4. Conscious Matter is the Body of Mind Energy

" I. Cosmic Matter is the Body of Cosmoenergy
" II. Cosmoenergy is the Body of Deific Energy
" III. Deific Energy is the Body of God
[and conversely for each]
" Time is the soul of space, etc." [26]

In such a hierarchal scheme God is a structural member — not a first cause or a directing will in control of the whole process. There is no process here, starting or ending in God, but rather a fixed and unchanging set of relationships in which God has his definite place.

Reuterdahl couches his ethics in the same individualistic language as his metaphysics. The Golden Rule becomes " the Gravitational Law of the Spiritual World," [27] acting in accord with " the Law of the Ascending Process." [28] One strongly suspects a conservative moralism in Reuterdahl, for having unleashed a blast against Freud for founding an analytical procedure that rests upon the most repulsive and indecent of inferences, he approvingly refers to D. H. Lawrence's description of Freud's cavern of dreams full of a huge slimy serpent of sex and heaps of excrement.[29]

Reuterdahl's mind may be imaginative, but it is hardly creative. It may build systems, but it hardly opens up new ideas. His thought is dependent upon the idea of an Absolute Universe, and in the name of an absolute universe he hurls considerable invective against the fourth-dimensional concept of Einstein. He regards modern mathematics as having developed an idea " that, for crass impossibility, is not excelled by any superstition charged to religion." [30] Why every thinking person knows that the world is a space of only three dimensions!

The sharp contrasts between Einstein and Reuterdahl are all too obvious. The one, a quiet scholar whose writings express a sense of reverent awe; the other, a writer of a sharply worded tract that claims to prove God. The one, a highly theoretical physicist whose thought defies the imagination; the other, a naïvely realistic scientist who expects scientific facts to meet the tests of common sense. And yet, both men have a type of religious orientation that stresses logical relationships, cosmic order, and the rational connections science builds between natural events. In both Einstein's cosmic religion and Reuterdahl's scientific cosmism, an identification has been found between the order of the cosmos and the idea of God.

This feeling for cosmic order is a foundation, however, for more than a cosmic mysticism or a scientific cosmism. It spills over, imperceptibly at first, and then more openly, into another type of religious philosophy. It becomes not in itself God, but the evidence of a prior reality, which is its first cause. When it does this, it makes closer contact with traditional religion, with a God of will and of purpose. It takes more account of the historical and personal element in the Godhead. To the story of this modification and extension of cosmic concern we next turn our attention.

II

CHRISTIAN THEISM:

GOD AS FIRST CAUSE

*" The scientist who recognizes God . . . feels that God is in na-
ture, that the orderly ways in which nature works are themselves
the manifestations of God's will and purpose. Its laws are His
orderly way of working."* [1] — Arthur Holly Compton.

THIS is the first of three chapters each of which deals
with a variation of Christian theism. They should be
looked at, not as separate and distinct types of religious philosophy, but as variations of a single type. Thus, this chapter deals with Christian theism emphasizing God as first
cause; the succeeding chapter, with a Christian theism seeking to work out the religious implications of evolution; the
third chapter, with Christian theism stressing the role of man
as a child of God. There is no reason, either historical or logical, why belief in God as first cause must exclude belief in
God as the author of an evolutionary process; there is every
reason to suppose that belief in God as first cause may go
hand in hand with a Christian humanism. But belief in God
as first cause, while not of itself an exclusive type of religious
philosophy, is, nevertheless, a distinct element (and in some
cases a distinct emphasis) in Christian theism, and it is to
this emphasis that we address ourselves here.

Belief in God as first cause — as the primary reality out of
which other reality springs — has as its starting point the
same awareness of an orderly nature as does belief in God as

a cosmic principle. However, God achieves his independence, so to speak, by virtue of the fact that he rules over the order of nature and is not bound to it or identified with it. The order of nature is a manifestation of God, not his essence or mode of being.

The Nobel prize-winning physicist, Dr. Arthur H. Compton, finds his strongest argument for God springing from the orderly character of the world. He asks, " Can it be a matter of chance that protons and photons and electrons have that particular set of characteristics that is necessary for development into a world of infinite variety and chance? " [2] He suggests at another place that " the argument on the basis of design, though trite, has never been adequately refuted." [3] He speaks of a " great unifying principle operating in all nature." [4]

Surely this is a religious awareness of an orderliness in nature. It finds this order pointing to God as its source and explanation; it believes in God as a first cause. It may use the vocabulary of cosmic religion, most particularly the term " Intelligence " as applied to God, and yet because it conceives of God in a different way, it adds the concept of purpose to the term, and speaks of " an Intelligence working in nature." [5] In this way it overcomes the idea of a remote, inflexible god and clears the way for a God at work in nature — not only as author and sustainer of the world, but as ruler and judge of the moral life of men.

Compton views God's relationship to the order of the cosmos as an overarching one. He affirms the validity of the God of Newton, a God known in the dependable order of nature. He criticizes the God of Laplace and Comte, a provisional and *ad hoc* explanation for events, the true mechanistic explanation of which is not known. In referring to Newton's God he notes, quoting Alfred Noyes,

" 'Tis not the lack of links within the chain,
From cause to cause, but that the chain exists,
That's the unfathomable mystery." [6]

The chain of order in nature becomes, in this view, the proof of God's existence above it.

This raises some problems concerning Compton's total religious outlook. In dealing with God he uses the idea of cosmic order. In dealing with the freedom of man, Compton uses Heisenberg's uncertainty principle as proof of a break in the tyranny of causality. He regards Heisenberg's case as having "been made so convincing that I should consider it more likely that the principle of the conservation of energy or the second law of thermodynamics should be found faulty than that we should return to a system of strict causality." [7] Is nature characterized by a chain of events, as Compton suggests when discussing God, or by uncertainty, as he suggests when dealing with the possible scientific collaboration of human freedom? Perhaps Compton would maintain that both orderliness and uncertainty characterize nature, that order comes in spite of the chance movement of atoms. But even this leaves unsolved problems: Why should the order of nature be used as an argument for God and the disorder an argument for human freedom? On what grounds — and perhaps to ask this question is merely to suggest the difficulties of drawing metaphysical consequences from physical analogies — would one be wrong in arguing against God on the basis of the Heisenberg principle and against human freedom on the basis of the causal chain in nature?

Compton's religious epistemology differs from both Einstein's sense of the unknowable and Reuterdahl's claim to have proved the existence of God. Compton draws an analogy between the method of science and that of religion. As unproved hypotheses exist in science, and even in science are taken on faith, so in religion hypotheses are legitimate and in no sense contradictory of scientific method. " Faith in God may be a thoroughly scientific attitude . . . based on the experience that the hypothesis of God gives a more reasonable interpretation of the world than any other." [8] Compton reserves a final judgment about faith in God, for the evidence may not yet be all in. He feels it is possible that

" [New] evidence will convince us that our faith that a God exists [is] wrong. It is more probable, however, as has nearly always been the case with so-called ' revolutions ' in science, that the new information will cause us to change in some way our conception of God." [9]

In the foregoing Compton raises as many problems as he solves, and his religious epistemology bears further scrutiny. Is tentative acceptance of a hypothesis an adequate faith in God? Does the scientific evidence of itself sustain faith in God, or does religious knowledge draw on other authority? Perhaps a clue to our further understanding at this point can be had by examining Compton's arguments with respect to belief in immortality. He suggests that belief in immortality is supported by two sets of reasons, one scientific and the other religious. The " scientific " reasons include the phenomenon of historical memory, the continuity of the race, and the fact that intelligent consciousness is the end product of the evolutionary process. The religious reasons include belief in the goodness of God, the infinite worth of character, the teaching of Jesus, and the witness of the resurrection. If immortality is, like faith in God, a hypothesis, then the justifications for the hypothesis put forth by Compton draw on both reason and traditional authority.

In this view experience and common sense are not decisive criteria of religious truth. This can be said, not because this is an explicit theological position that demands revealed truth, but because in various arguments for religious ideas it

draws upon human experience in various, and even contradictory, ways. For example, let us compare two statements regarding the role of common sense.

"It takes but little investigation to find that . . . faith
in the completeness of physical death is usually based upon
an uncritical acceptance of a common sense realism, similar to that which accepts a brick as the hard, heavy, red
object that can be held in the hands. Just as a careful examination shows the brick to consist of a group of mole-
cules, atoms, and electrons — a complex system wholly
different from the common sense picture — so the 'obvious-
ness' of death is found to disappear when more closely
studied." [10]

The impact of the above statement is exactly reversed by
the following:

"Even if logic appeared to favor determinism, as it has
at many stages of our scientific knowledge, I should be
unable to avoid a strong skepticism of a conclusion so contrary to the dictates of common sense." [11]

There is an ambiguity here regarding the relationship of
common sense to religious truth. Christian faith holds to belief in immortality; in speaking of immortality Compton denies the meaning of common sense. Christian faith believes
in human freedom; in speaking of human freedom Compton
bases the case mostly upon common sense. That Compton
consistently holds to his religious tenets, even at the price
of an inconsistent attitude toward experience, shows how
crucially religious tradition affects his total outlook.

Man's role in the cosmos receives great emphasis in Compton's thought. Man lives in an orderly universe. He must attune himself to nature's laws or be broken against them.
"Such is the stern yet kindly dictum which science has to
offer." [12] This demand is likewise found in the Biblical
phrases, "All things work together for good to them that love

God " and " The wages of sin is death."

But this is not a deterministic picture. It is rather a picture of a world whose orderliness is the context in which man can himself work as part of an eternal purpose. " Up to the dawn of social conscience . . . ," Compton writes, " God held in his own hands the whole responsibility for the evolution of life upon this planet. Gradually this responsibility is being shifted to our shoulders." [13] This is an interesting way of phrasing it. Does God abdicate in favor of man? Certainly not! Compton, as the context of this phrase shows us, is enthusiastic about the tremendous scientific and spiritual achievements of civilizations. Through science man increasingly partakes of God's purpose. Before science and civilization, God alone controlled the natural world. Now, man shares this power and responsibility. This does not rule God out; it brings man in — into the thrilling prospects of a concretely expressed sonship of the divine, into a freedom that comes from knowledge of the law-abiding character of the universe.

Here is a humanism based, not on man's isolated attempt to construct a system of values in an impartial world, but rather on man's capacity to partake of the whole Purpose that rules the cosmos. This is a thrilling prospect for Compton; he rejoices in it as follows:

" Considering the many obvious errors that we are making we may be thankful that we do not yet have complete control. Yet who can fail to respond to the opportunity and challenge that are before us of working with the God of the universe in carrying through the final stages of making this a suitable world and ourselves a suitable race for what is perhaps the supreme position of intelligent life in his world! " [14]

In partaking of the ethical purpose of the universe, man must be primarily motivated by love: " The gradual evolution of conscience implies the survival value of the altruism implied by good will"; [15] "It is becoming increasingly difficult [because of the advance of science] in either political or economic life for any individual or group to justify breeding of antagonisms on the basis of selfish interest"; [16] "Once again, as in the days of the Roman Empire, society is ripe for a renewed emphasis on the spirit of service for the common welfare of man." [17]

In terms of specific policy Compton's attitudes stand in almost complete contrast to those of Einstein. Einstein has strong affinities for socialism and was once a clear-cut pacifist. Compton on the other hand willingly took a role in the development of the atomic bomb, and gives frequent expression to his opposition to excessive governmental control of either science or economics. He writes, "The greater part of our own scientific work during the past generation has been made possible because in America individual business enterprise has been encouraged by large rewards." [18]

Compton represents a not unusual combination of Christian love and American optimistic good will. His idea of Christian love as the spirit of altruism working in individual members of society has fallen into disrepute. It is undeniably bland for the struggles of an atomic age, and it too often sanctions the substitution of pious charity for a righteous concern for social justice. Compton's ethic is dated.

The onetime director of the Detroit Observatory of the University of Michigan, Heber D. Curtis, has many of the same outlooks toward religion as does Dr. Compton. "My cosmos *must* be orderly," [19] he writes. This starting point is much like Compton's. Curtis goes on, suggesting that religion consists of two elements: (1) the assumption of a Higher Power (distinct from the cosmos, but evidenced in it and in control of it), and (2) the effort of man to attune himself to this Power. Assumption, hypothesis, highly probable explanation — these are the terms in which religion is described.

" No theory of this cosmos can be adequate which does not give some theory or hypothesis for the occurrence of these two remarkable factors [mind or personality], [purpose and gradual development]. I personally can conceive no hypothesis for all this which seems so simple and satisfactory, so adequate, so in accord with existing methods of scientific inference, as those conclusions which we commonly term religion." [20]

Thus religion is justified as hypothesis, as speculation regarding the transcendental and unknowable. Curtis, like Compton, points to the fact, that " science . . . is in every field making speculations, or holding beliefs as working hypotheses. . . . Science certainly has no right to refuse others the privileges which it is constantly and implicitly assuming for itself." [21]

Anthony Standen, a Brooklyn College chemist, has written recently a pungent best seller, *Science Is a Sacred Cow*. Its purpose is to explode a bomb under scientism, the worship of scientific technique, and not to develop a religious philosophy. However, it contains many statements about religious matters and bears scrutiny here.

Following Plato's *Republic* in saying that knowledge may be schematized on a divided line, Standen suggests:

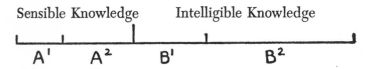

A^1 = mirages (where our senses deceive us)
A^2 = the real world of things

$B^1 =$ the world of mathematics, equal in length to A^2 to signify that it fits A^2

$B^2 =$ higher knowledge (God) [22]

His religious concern appears when he criticizes scientists for having no notion of what goes on in section B^2. This leads them, as Standen sees it, to pursue science either for its utilitarian value or for its own sake, whereas " the first purpose of science is to learn about God, and admire Him, through His handiwork." [23] Thus the idea of God is bound with the idea of an orderly nature.

But God is not equated with this order; he is its author. " The [laws of nature] are God's laws," [24] and " even if purpose in nature could be explained as ' chance association of atoms ' . . . there is still a very big question to be asked, that of where, on earth or in heaven, such wonderful atoms could have come from? " [25] This is explicit belief in God as first cause.

Standen is careful to distinguish between this idea and the suggestion that God is an explanation for things we don't yet know. " He underlies all the areas [of knowledge], both those that are ' explained ' by science and those that are not." [26]

" [To use God to explain the things we don't know is] poor theology and thoroughly rotten science. It is poor theology because as more and more things become ' explained ' by science, God would get smaller and smaller! It is rotten science because it is not the business of science to go back to first causes: proximate causes are the proper field of science, and if we haven't found the proximate causes the thing to say is just that we haven't yet found the proximate causes." [27]

That Standen looks at God as a first cause is further evidenced in his insistence that God is free, not subject to predictability by human analysis. He ridicules Lundberg (*Can*

Science Save Us?) for the suggestion that scientific tech-
niques can predict the choices of men and even the choices
of God. "Even the law knows better," Standen says. "An
act of God is, legally, 'an event which no man could have
foreseen.'" [28]

Turning to man as related to God, Standen continues his
blistering ridicule of determinism. "Instances of the almost
unpredictability of man are known to the social scientists,"
he writes, "but they are no more affected by them than the
asylum inmate is by being told he is not Napoleon." [29] Man
is a thinking animal, and this marks him as different from the
other animals. Man is hungry for knowledge, for certainty.
This is the driving force behind science itself, and it is not
to be understood in mechanistic terms.

Beyond this, however, Standen's conception of man and his
relation to God is not so fully spelled out as that of Compton
or of Einstein. Standen would not oppose all the constructive human activity in which man is engaged, but one feels
that he is really concerned that man should worship God.
As Standen sees it, the first purpose of science is "to learn
about God, and admire Him, through His handiwork. If any
usefulness comes in — as it does in large quantities — why,
so much the better." [30]

Taking an example now from a man writing at the turn of
the century, we find in Professor William North Rice, geologist at Connecticut Wesleyan University, a man who turned
the idea of God as first cause into a powerful witness to his
Christian faith. As his friends have noted in tribute, Professor
Rice took a crucial role in relating Christianity to the intellectual climate of modern science.[31] His book *Christian Faith
in an Age of Science,* written as it was at the turn of the century, had more historical significance at its time than it has
now. Nevertheless, it evidences an acute mind wrestling with

the relationship between science and religion and arriving at many insights that sound familiar to us today.

"Natural law and providence are not," writes Professor Rice, "as men have fancied, conceptions contradictory and mutually exclusive. Law and providence are only two phases of the same truth." [32] The conception of God starts with the recognition of an orderly cosmos; it does not, however, stop with this, but goes on; "if all events in nature obey the will of intelligent personality, then all events in nature are purposeful." [33]

That one of Rice's contemporary concerns was to refute deism colors his work. He speaks of a theology "relieved of the awkward notion of a benevolent Deity spending an eternity in solitude and idleness." [34] He uses a phrase much like Compton's "chain of causes." "God dwells in a continuity of nature, not in imaginary gaps." [35] Passages in Rice stress the changelessness of God and the uniformity of nature in such close relationship that one is tempted to suggest that Rice has a cosmic religion. He says, for example, "The unity of the cosmos proclaims indubitably the unity of that cause in which the cosmos has its being," [36] or again: "God is everywhere or nowhere in the universe. He does everything or nothing. All philosophical theists must hold that the cause of the uniformities of nature is to be found in the will of an immanent Intelligence, whose plans are changeless because his wisdom is perfect from all eternity." [37]

Rice frankly faces the possibility that this is pantheism. He argues that it is only a phase of pantheism, since it includes a place for the personality of God. "We find the ground of all existence in the will of a personal God." "Pantheism denies personality, free will, morality, alike in man and God." [38] Thus Rice applies the terms personality and purpose to God. He is a Christian theist.

Many of Rice's formulations will strike responsive chords

with contemporary theologians. For example, Rice denies the mind-body dualism on which much Christian theology in this century has based its case for both freedom of the will and belief in the immortality of the soul. In dealing with the problem of freedom Rice suggests his belief in self-determination as opposed to mere freedom of the soul, and in discussing immortality he writes:

"It is a profoundly significant fact that Christianity, with Judaism and Mohammedanism, which are respectively incomplete and corrupted phases of Christianity, stands alone among the religions and the philosophies of the world in teaching an embodied immortality. It is not the immortality of a disembodied spirit that Paul preached on the Areopagus amid the scoffs of Athenian philosophers, but resurrection." [39]

Rice's philosophical speculation makes frequent reference to the Biblical message. At times there is a glimpse of a dialectical attitude toward Biblical truth, as when Rice suggests that "while the legend of the fall passes away, the doctrine of the Fall remains." [40] Suggestions along such lines indicate that Rice is struggling to reconcile Christian faith with scientific facts. He is wrestling with the meaning of Christian faith and the possibility of Christian faith in an age of science, and, as the tributes to him tell us, his work along these lines was of tremendous help to the students who studied under him.

Rice was not, however, a Biblical theologian; he was a liberal Christian theist, more concerned to avoid the Biblicism of his day than to avoid its rationalism. He bases his discussion on philosophical considerations. His attitude toward the Bible and his definition of religion are those of a liberal thinker.

"We may find in the Bible the story of the origin of Christianity. But the Bible is not, as it has sometimes been falsely said to be, our religion. Religion is not a book. Religion is the intellectual acceptance of truth in regard to the relations of God and man. Religion is the emotional response of the soul to truth accepted. Religion is the voluntary fulfillment of the duties which that truth demands. Religion is faith and love and life." [41]

Imperceptibly at first, and then with an overwhelming crescendo, the idea of God as first cause moves to the idea of God as continual cause — as an ever-present reality causing growth. This view takes the scientific idea of evolution and makes it the basis not alone of scientific fact but of religious meaning. Loosely speaking, it is a religious view of God as growth. To the many variations of this new theme we now turn our attention.

III

CHRISTIAN THEISM:

Emphasis Upon the Idea of Growth

" The discovery of radioactivity in 1896 has revealed an entirely new property of matter and quite as important a property, so far as its influence upon our conception of our world is concerned, as any which has ever been discovered. For it forced us, for the first time, to begin to think in terms of a universe which is changing, living, growing, even in its elements — a dynamic instead of a static universe. It has exerted the most profound influence not only upon physics, which gave it birth, but also upon chemistry, upon geology, upon biology, upon philosophy. Indeed, it is at this point that one of the great contributions of science to religion is now being made."— Robert Andrews Millikan.[1]

IN THE early 1920's conservative religious forces, upholding a doctrine of creation based upon a literal reading of Genesis, were vigorously attacking the biological theory of evolution with a misguided zeal that was to break out in the bitterness of the Scopes trial of 1925. The controversy appeared to the public as an irreconcilable clash between science and religion. To alleviate this feeling a group of thirty-five, mostly clergymen and scientists, issued a *Joint Statement Upon the Relation of Science and Religion*. It said:

" We, the undersigned, deeply regret that in recent controversies there has been a tendency to present science and religion as irreconcilable and antagonistic domains of thought, for in fact they meet distinct human needs, and in the rounding out of human life they supplement rather than displace or oppose each other.

"*The purpose of science is to develop, without preju-dice or preconceptions of any kind, a knowledge of the facts, the laws, and the processes of nature. The even more important task of religion, on the other hand, is to develop the consciences, the ideals, and the aspirations of mankind.* Each of these two activities represents a deep and vital function of the soul of man, and both are necessary for the life, the progress, and the happiness of the human race.

"It is a sublime conception of God which is furnished by science, and one wholly consonant with the highest ideals of religion, when it represents him as revealing him-self through countless ages in the development of the earth as an abode for man and in the agelong inbreathing of life into its constituent matter, culminating in man with his spiritual nature and all his godlike powers." [2]

This joint statement reflects an emphasis that was to play a crucial role in the liberal Christian theism of our century. Actually, though the distinction between them may some-times be blurred, the evolutionary concept was to be used in two ways. In the first case, the scientific conception of a changing, growing, evolving universe became a singular proof of God — a witness to his orderly control of nature. In such instances the general framework of Christian theism is unaltered; God himself is unchanging and eternal, the ruler of process. In the second case, evolution becomes a clue to the nature of God. The classic formulation of this alternative is Alfred North Whitehead's philosophy of organ-ism, in which the concept of process occupies so large a part. The idea of growth is used as a metaphysical principle for the interpretation of all reality.

In the first group we come to Henry Fairfield Osborn, former professor of zoology at Columbia and past president of the American Museum of Natural History. Osborn is mainly concerned with defending the teaching of evolution. His book *Evolution and Religion in Education* [3] is a spirited defense of the teaching of evolution as a scientific truth. With this concern he couples a constant emphasis that evolution is not antagonistic to religion. While he may have wished to crusade merely for the freedom of science, Osborn found himself in the thick of theological controversy. How tense the feelings were at the time is portrayed in this autobiographical note:

"I recently delivered at New Haven a perfectly innocent address on the Origin of the Species; in it there was not a word about religion, but when it bore the headlines imprint it appeared in all parts of the United States as 'Osborn Raps Traditional Theology' or 'Osborn Declares Science and Religion Irreconcilable.'" [4]

Osborn tried to show that evolution enhances our conception of God's majesty. Suggesting first that evolution is distinct from revolution — even opposed to it — he goes on to point out: "Revolution destroys the good with the bad. Evolution destroys the bad and favors the good. Revolution occurs again and again in the mind and heart of man. Evolution begins and ends with the purposes of God." [5] "Evolution by no means takes God out of the universe, but it greatly increases both the wonder, the mystery, and the marvelous order which we call 'Natural Law' pervading all nature." [6]

Osborn regarded the Bible as a history of the spiritual and moral progress of man — much as does Harry Emerson Fosdick in his *A Guide to Understanding the Bible*. Also, he refers to Saint Augustine as having "a thoroughly modern theistic conception of evolution," [7] inasmuch as Augustine recognizes all development to take place under God's providence. These are parts of an attempt to find a meeting ground for science and religion — they are not (at least in their main context) part of a new interpretation of religion based on evolution. Osborn sought a religion that could live with the doctrine of evolution — a scientific theory he regarded as indisputably established, that is, "a natural law."

A younger contemporary of Osborn, a signer of the joint statement and a well-known scientist, made evolution into a principle of interpretation of both science and religion. Robert Andrews Millikan, whose name is highly esteemed in the world of physics, has been a productive writer on religious matters from the point of view of a Christian theist. He starts his conception of God with the idea of order, but to it he adds the idea of development. The union of these two into the idea of orderly development plays an important role in Millikan's thought. He suggests that the conception of progress is "the most sublime, the most stimulating conception that has ever entered human thought." [8] He maintains that *"two great influences . . . have made goodness the outstanding characteristic in the conception of God. The first influence was Jesus of Nazareth; the second influence has been the growth of modern science, and particularly the growth of the theory of evolution."* [9]

These two aspects of nature, order and growth, are fused in Millikan's idea of God. God is an agent working through the order of nature and furthering a progressive change. The scientific idea of law-abiding growth changes man's idea of God from that of a capricious deity to that of a "vital agent in the march of things." [10] In Galileo's work, and the science of celestial mechanics that flowed from it, Millikan finds mankind's idea of God enriched. Law and development become inseparable in God, and order is essential to change.

Millikan's philosophical bias is idealistic in the technical sense of attaching great importance to the place of mind and thought. Perhaps he would be cautious in identifying himself with any given philosophical school; his point about the place of ideas and human thoughts does not carry through the logic as rigidly as this would demand. Nevertheless he is able to say:

> " In the final analysis, the thing in this world which is of most supreme importance, indeed the thing which is of most practical value to the race, is not, after all, useful discovery or invention, but that which lies far back of them, namely, ' the way men think.' " [11]

Millikan regards the mind, the very fact that it exists at all, as the most amazing thing in all life.

He often employs the word " idea " or " spirit " when speaking of religion. Two crucial revolutions in thought, on which the whole modern conception of religion and life is based, are the " *idea* of progress " and the " *idea* of responsibility." The first of these is the contribution of science, springing from the recognition of an orderly universe; the second is the " ought " of religion, springing most clearly from the Golden Rule. The " ought " of religion has come to us as a result of an evolutionary process; " religion itself is one of the most striking possible examples of evolution." [12] It will exist as long as man " hopes, aspires, and reflects upon the meaning of existence and the responsibilities that it entails." [13]

Millikan's contrast between science and religion is based on the Kantian dualism of physical and moral knowledge. This appears again in the suggestion made in Millikan's autobiography, that human well-being and progress rest on two pillars: " the spirit of science " and " the spirit of religion." But if there is this strict dualism, why the effort to emphasize the parallel character of both religion and science? Indeed, is it possible to conceive of evolution in religion after the pattern of evolution in biology? Are there not two levels here, one on which facts can be empirically gathered, another on which duty is categorical?

Moreover, is it possible to regard religion as developing in a clear pattern? The concept of spiritual progress has undergone rude shocks in recent decades. It might even be possible to suggest that Communism represents a "late" form of religion, but surely Millikan would not regard it as a high expression of spirituality.

Another problem concerning this evolutionary view of religion is raised when Millikan stops with a particular religion as a fitting object for his own devotion. Millikan is a liberal Christian. But why stop here? A logical evolutionary pattern might well be argued to take place in the movement from polytheism to monotheism to nontheism: from many gods, to one God, to no god. Surely, within the concept of evolution itself there is no basis for justifying a mid-point in the chain. Only from the standpoint of ethical monotheism is ethical monotheism the fitting outcome of an evolutionary process.

Perhaps Millikan comes closer to humanism than appears at first sight. If religion is an "idea," it may indeed be a human idea and ultimately dependent upon man. If ethical fulfillment is shifted to man, upon whom the march of progress comes ultimately to depend, is there room left for the redemptive significance of God?

How strongly Millikan emphasizes the human element in religion is impressed upon the reader again and again. He suggests at one point, applying to men the same phrase — "vital agents in the march of things" — he has earlier applied to God, that

"by definitely introducing the most stimulating and inspiring motive for altruistic effort which has ever been introduced, namely, the motive arising from the conviction that we ourselves may be vital agents in the march of things, science has provided a reason for altruistic effort which is quite independent of the ultimate destination of the individual and is also much more alluring to some sorts of minds than that of singing hosannas forever around the throne." [14]

But what of the content of this effort? Millikan calls it " altruistic." He ties it to the teachings of Christ, perhaps forgetting that higher criticism had raised many issues regarding the accuracy and completeness of the New Testament account of these teachings. Thus " *it is the life and the teachings of Jesus which constitute all that is essential to Christianity, that the spread of his spirit of unselfishness, of his idealism, and of his belief in the brotherhood of man and the fatherhood of God is the great purpose of the Christian religion.*" [15] In practice the application of these teachings involves a cautious liberalism, not a revolutionary zeal. Evolution is not revolution, any more than it is stagnation.

" The man of education and intelligence in general joins neither the conventional crowd which simply passes on the past without change . . . nor the red mob, the devotees of the next easiest and cheapest philosophy." [16]

We must " supplement, extend, build over a bit our old theories, not abandon them." [17] There is no blanket sanction for revolution in the idea of growth and development. In fact, orderly development involves the maintaining of as much as is valid and usable and permanently true in the old.

While scientific determinism (not to be confused with philosophic determinism) may be " a convenient working hypothesis," [18] man is a free agent. " Practical free will, or the sense of responsibility, is a brute fact given by direct experience." [19] It is this freedom of man that makes possible the altruistic enterprise, which makes it possible for each individual to follow the dictates of his conscience. Here again, Millikan is seeking to distinguish between scientific and religious realms at the same time that he is seeking to establish, within the idea of evolution, a similarity between them.

There is no hint of a challenge to social structures in Mil-

likan's writings. The Church is to inject into human society
"the sense of social responsibility, the spirit of altruism, of
service, of brotherly love, of Christlikeness." [20] Or more directly put, speaking at the award of a gram of radium to
Madame Curie, he says:

> "Finally, the most significant thing about this evening
> is the way in which this contribution to further progress
> has been made: not through a public grant — that is not
> the method through which the genius of Anglo-Saxon
> civilization has ever expressed itself, but rather through
> private initiative." [21]

Millikan's is a hopeful philosophy; it is probably a typically American version of Christianity, very much on the
wane in a crisis era. Its real metaphysical roots are in the idea
of evolution, in the idea of growth — translated into a complete and optimistic view of life for man. The flavor of Millikan's thought may be strange in an uneasy age, but the
attempt to deal with religion in response to a creative understanding of evolution is a recurrent theme among the scientists.

Such a philosophy orientated in the idea of evolution has
recurred in a particularly well-stated form in the thought of
Lecomte du Noüy. Du Noüy is French by birth and upbring-
ing, but in his late years moved to America, where he wrote
his best seller, *Human Destiny*.[22] This book is his most significant work and represents as carefully a thought-out religious system based on the idea of evolution as has appeared
from the pen of a scientist. Millikan has termed it, "a book
of such fundamental grasp and insight as cannot be expected
to appear more than once or twice in a century," a very gen-
erous comment from a kindred mind.

Du Noüy terms his thought "telefinalism"; the term involves aspects of thought in the ideas of both first cause and

evolution. Du Noüy suggests:

"Telefinality orients the march of evolution as a whole, and has acted, ever since the appearance of life on earth, as a distant directing force tending to develop a being endowed with a conscience, a spiritually and morally perfect being. To attain its goal, this force acts on the laws of the inorganized world in such a way that the normal play of the second law of thermodynamics is always deflected in the same direction, a direction forbidden to inert matter and leading to ever greater dissymmetries, ever more 'improbable' states." [23]

There are several distinct ideas involved in this summary, which Du Noüy elaborates in the course of his argument. There is the idea of a goal: Telefinalism postulates the "intervention of an Idea, a Will, a supreme Intelligence." [24] The need to conceive of such a reality — God — cannot be concretized (Einstein's anthropomorphizing) but can never be overcome. Science cannot answer the final question of cause, and we thus, if we probe deeply enough, "automatically arrive at the First Cause, and the problem passes imperceptibly from the material realm into the philosophical and religious realms." [25]

"Evolution," according to Du Noüy, ". . . is comprehensible only if we admit that it is dominated by a finality, a precise and distant goal." [26] This is because evolution can be shown by (1) mathematical probability computations, and (2) the irreversibility of material process to stand in sharp contrast with inorganic process. Du Noüy suggests that two things about evolution show the bankruptcy of materialistic interpretations of reality. Evolution would have taken place only if the cosmos was governed by an "antichance," which positively speaking implies the idea of God; evolution can continue to take place only by defying the running-down character of the inorganic world.

Thus, evolution is not adaptation, but freedom. Adaptation leads to the end of any species that merely fits itself to the environment. Pre-Cambrian sandworms adapted themselves to life better than man; they died. Adaptation is guided by the criterion of usefulness — and those who take its way become not only clumsy and troublesome, but even "harmful monstrosities."[27] The law of evolution, however, is liberty. It involves the choice for forms of higher potentiality. It means becoming more creative (and therefore more unstable) organisms. Man has emerged as the highest of such organisms, with the liberty of his mind and will. It is because man stands over and against the inorganic world that he represents the high achievement of evolution.

Evolution is at a halfway point: it "continues in our time, no longer on the physiological or anatomical plane but on the spiritual and moral plane."[28] Man now must assert his freedom and grow. "Henceforth, contrary to all the other [species], in order to evolve *he must no longer obey nature.*"[29] Here Du Noüy becomes a humanist in the sense of finding in man the ongoing development that leads to the goal of evolution. God is not ruled out, as in naturalistic or nontheistic humanism; indeed, God is the goal, the guide, under which man will grow and to whom man must be obedient. But the task is man's. It is a struggle of great moment, by which man himself is changed, not merely the contraptions and tools he uses. This struggle may be temporarily forced down, in which case the growing and improving remnant may have to hibernate, but we have in Christ a token that it can be done.

"Christ did not come too soon, for only the example of infinite perfection and total sacrifice could inspire men with the ambition to improve themselves and with the hope of resembling him one day."[30]

This raises a question as to whether Du Noüy has taken the problem of evil with full seriousness. The idea of evolution is taken from the biological realm; Du Noüy recognizes that in applying it to the realm of freedom he makes a radical step. He suggests that evolution involves, not the survival of the fittest brutes, but the freedom of organism to choose ever higher forms of potentiality. But if freedom is to be truly freedom, must it not be possible for man to defeat evolution, not merely give it a temporary setback? Is not the realm of history one in which man has freedom to defy evolution, and incidentally, is he not precariously close to the possibility of exercising this freedom?

It is apparent throughout his whole book that Du Noüy is wrestling for a basis of agreement between science and religion. He is often critical of a "scientifically outdated materialistic faith," [31] springing from the fact that "the prestige of science amongst men is also a kind of superstition." [32] He finds that there can be no contradiction between the facts of science and religion. He pleads for a high and stanch allegiance to the moral law. He speaks reverently and carefully of the Christian faith and Christian institutions. He has made a full and unique attempt to base theism upon an interpretation of the meaning of evolution.

An interesting variation of the idea of development as a basis of religious faith was contributed by Michael Pupin. He called it "creative co-ordination" or the movement from chaos to cosmos. "Modern science," he writes, "shows that all terrestrial organisms are endowed with a power of co-ordination which transforms the chaotic, the noncoordinated, forms of energy radiated to us by the sun into co-ordinated forms." [33] "Cosmic energy, generated in tenuous and intensely active substance of the young stars, moves from chaos to cosmos." [34]

Pupin found this formula applicable and germane not only to an understanding of the wider cosmos in Christian terms

but also to man's place in the cosmos and to man's understanding of it. Creative co-ordination will lift the life of humanity from chaos to cosmos — to the Kingdom of God.[35]
History proves that spiritual co-ordinating forces are the
most powerful co-ordinating forces, more powerful than
physical ones.[36] " I firmly believe that the co-ordinating
power of those [scientific men discovering truths about na-
ture] was derived from being in tune with messages which
are broadcasted from that great station which is the fountain
of the eternal truth." [37]

We are examining Pupin's addition of a new term to the
literature of those philosophies finding religious significance
in the idea of growth, process, and development. Pupin applies the term to the cosmic picture — as an explanation of
the whole of nature; he applies it to man's place in the cosmos and his means of understanding it; he applies it also to
a simple statement of ethical or moral idealism.

" When the vague moral principles of the many creeds
and civilizations were co-ordinated and summed up in
the words of a single sentence, ' Love thy neighbor as thy-
self,' the Christian world recognized in it a transcendent
power of co-ordination, a heavenly harmony, which cannot originate in the soul of a mere mortal man, and hence
our firm Christian belief that its possessor, our Lord Jesus
Christ, is the Son of God." [38]

The liberal Christian theism discussed in the last two
chapters has again and again moved from the question of
God to a consideration of the significance of man. Compton,
Millikan, and Du Noüy, to mention the obvious examples, have
all approached a humanism based upon man's partnership
with the divine. This tendency may become even stronger,
until the emphasis upon man becomes the major preoccupa-
tion of a thinker and the role of man, the crucial aspect of

religious faith. When this occurs without the context of Christian theism, it dissolves God and leaves man alone to give meaning and purpose to life. But when it occurs within the framework of Christian theism, a new emphasis develops in which the ethical and moral aspects of Christianity become central, moral achievement becomes primary, and man's role as a child of God becomes the essential feature of the Christian faith.

IV

CHRISTIAN THEISM:

Emphasis Upon Man's Role in Religion

" To the reverent scientist . . . the simplest features of the world about us are in themselves so awe-inspiring that there seems no need to seek new and greater miracles as evidences of God's care. The truly vital feature of religion is the profound meaning which it attaches to life and the demand which it places on our loyalties and affections." [1]
" The fruitfulness of religion as an agency for human progress depends on its own ability to meet the changing needs of each new generation." [2] — Carl Wallace Miller.

WE COME now to a type of religious outlook that in philosophical jargon we might describe as theistic humanism. Many would regard this phrase as a contradiction of terms, but it need not be. By it we may convey the idea of a religious outlook that accepts belief in God as an essential part of religion, but places emphasis upon the aspiration and devotion of man. In it, the service of human need becomes the crucial and essentially significant criterion of religious meaning.

Such distinctions as exist between the three emphases of Christian theism must be understood as variations within a common set of assumptions. In this chapter we meet ideas that in many respects would be accepted by all Christian theists, and yet, because the individuals here place particular emphasis upon man, they come to judge religion in terms of its capacity to serve human need. They reinterpret many aspects of Christian faith.

Kirtley Mather, Harvard geologist, comes within this group. He has a great deal to say about God, yet what he says never appears as a carefully thought out and highly philosophical argument for God's existence. It is more apt to be a personal testimony.

" Knowledge concerning God, therefore, becomes a matter of human experience which includes both contact with the physical world of sense perception in which he is the motive power, and also direct, though mysterious, contact with him, when spirit meets with Spirit." [3]

Behind the universe there is a motivating power, which " the scientist calls universal energy, or what he is learning to call cosmic mind, or [to] what some of us would prefer to apply the old name, God." [4] Mather is skeptical of all attempts to define or describe God; such attempts are destined to fail, for " we cannot even approximate a satisfactory description or definition of that which is infinite and that of which so much is unknowable." [5] Mather confesses that he is left cold by Jeans's suggestion that the universe is more like a mathematical thought than like a machine. He finally finds God in Jesus Christ, since Christ reveals " the true character of the administration of the universe." [6]

This religious epistemology is based on a distinction between the measurable and the immeasurable in nature. Of the " half dozen questions which stimulate the activity of the human mind: what, where, when, who, how, and why . . . science answers only the first five." [7] Empirical religion answers the sixth.

Theology is a science because it assumes working hypotheses. The religious hypothesis is that we can interpret the reality of the unseen correctly, and that there are uniform spiritual laws. Hence, religion is a further extension of science; religion is the science of immeasurable values.

" The wise theologian is also a scientist. Applying the

test of pragmatism, he asks the question, 'How does it work, what are the results in human lives of each possible interpretation of the experience under consideration?'" [8]
Religion is a human activity. It grows and evolves. It is known by its fruits. The theologian will constantly be revising, rooting out error, destroying in order to construct. "Unless [the scientific method] is applied to the problems of religion, the theologian cannot expect to make any permanent gains in the midst of modern civilization." [9]

An empirical religious knowledge of God precludes both pantheism and deism. "Spiritual realities may be recognized only by their products." [10] Therefore, nature can only reveal God's activity and cannot of itself be identified with God. On the other hand, science in its knowledge of the natural world leaves a deistic god no place to dwell. The orderliness and impartiality of nature's laws are a manifestation of God, neither in themselves God nor in themselves independent of him. Thus God is both immanent and transcendent. In Mather's words:

"God is a power, immanent in the universe. He is involved in the hazard of his creation. He is striving mightily to produce a perfect display in the world of sense perception, of his own true nature." [11]

Nevertheless:

"Not all the resources of the universe are today in use, even as many now used were not in use a geologic period ago. In other words, the theistic God is not only immanent, he is transcendent." [12]

To consider more carefully the implications of Mather's religious empiricism, rather than its specific conclusions about God's nature, is to discover a strong reliance and emphasis upon the place of man in the discovery and development of religious knowledge. "The problem concerning the nature of God is in a very real sense," Mather writes, "coin-

cident with the problem concerning the nature of man." [13]
Man searches for religious truth; the search itself has religious significance. In seeking God man raises his own spirit to new heights.

Thus, prayer "not only reacts psychologically to benefit the one who prays; it also puts at the disposal of the Transcendent Spirit a tool which, however weak or tiny it may be, is nevertheless indispensable in the project of creating a world which will be an adequate expression of the nature of God." [14] It is this stress on man, both as the one who seeks God and the one who responds in faith to God, that makes Mather's thought an example of Christian humanism.

In his ethics Mather makes logical and direct deductions from his metaphysics. " For the insect society the motto seems to be ' One for all '; for the human society, which we are trying to perfect, the motto is not simply ' One for all ' but also ' All for one.' " [15] Mankind is collectively in charge of his world, but only as he respects the laws of the spirit can he survive. In respecting these laws mankind will gain eternal life. The chief concern of religion becomes " the moral quality of the universe." Here moral considerations overcome cosmological ones. " Immortality is an achievement to be won, not a gift to be accepted." [16] Man ought to share and distribute justly the wealth of the physical world; of this, there is, as Mather suggests in the title of one of his books, *Enough and to Spare*. In distributing the resources of the earth humanity will find a balanced and abundant life. Its co-operation will achieve justice for all. The planned, purposeful, and deliberate achievements of man take a central place in such an ethic.

A more explicitly humanistic type of religious outlook — though one still stated in Christian terms and postulating a belief in God — is to be found in Carl Wallace Miller's book,

A Scientist's Approach to Religion.[17] This Brown University physics professor approaches God through moral rather than cosmic considerations. The first of the great commandments, " Thou shalt love the Lord thy God," becomes for him " an exhortation to adjust oneself sympathetically to the realities of cosmic law." [18] We are to act as though God exists. Since there are evidences that the universe is orderly, " belief in God is acceptance of the basic principle that the universe makes sense, that there is behind it an ultimate purpose." [19] Belief in God, having this ethical quality of acceptance, changes daily living; it " becomes a creative force for advancing the cause of humanity." [20] Thus, belief in God is tested and vindicated by its social consequences. As Miller points out at one place,

> " The acceptance or nonacceptance of the principles of cosmic purposes as a guide to human activities must be decided in the final analysis by its promise of fruitfulness." [21]

And at another point:

> " Given two alternative hypotheses of equal likelihood, science would always select that which promised to be most fruitful. Can we question the benefits which have accrued to humanity from a sincere belief in divine Providence? May we not still set our courses by the stars? " [22]

The idea of God becomes a hypothesis that is tested, not by its congruence with an external or factual reality, but by the effect upon human behavior that it produces.

This carries with it immediate ethical implications; it may even be suggested that in this view religion becomes an ethical enterprise, with the individual attuning himself to the cosmic order and acting responsibly because he believes that God exists. Prayer becomes " an adjustment of one's own life and purposes to the will of divine Providence." [23] It is not a way to change the requirements of the moral law or to affect

the inexorable happenings of the natural order. The cross of
Christ becomes the supreme moral power.

"The crowning glory of human society is to be found
in the willingness of its noblest members, once a moral issue has been adequately defined, to 'set their faces stead-
fastly toward Jerusalem.' Thus it is neither an accident or
a consequence of a religious theory that the cross of Christ
has become a universal symbol of the sacrificial devotion
of human kind at its best." [24]

"Herein is to be found the power of the cross as a revolutionary force for human betterment." [25]

Man's ability to follow a religion of this kind — to be a
responsible agent in an ethical enterprise — is predicated on
the idea of free will. Without free will the entire structure of
religion collapses. Free will is not just random freedom, but
the ability to modify human destiny by human choice. The
modification occurs within the limits of a given environment.
A compromise is possible between the ideas of absolute freedom and absolute determinism, even as in physics the laws
of Newton and the quantum theory may both be applicable,
but under different conditions.

Miller is hostile toward any religious ideas that might undercut human effort. He criticizes the idea of an eternal reward in a heavenly future because it becomes an escape from
present tasks. He notes that "Jesus never gave cause for belief that even his own sacrifice on the cross could by any process of mental gymnastics serve as a substitute for man's fulfillment of his obligation to society." [26] With regard to the
eschatological expectation of a possible end to history he
remarks:

"The revelation of God's bountiful provision for mankind as found in the physical world . . . combined with
the demonstration written into the pages of history of the
moral and idealistic possibilities of the human species at

its best should go far toward acquitting divine Providence
of such gloomy intentions [as letting mankind be destroyed
in a cataclysm]," [27]
and dealing with the theme even more caustically:

"It is worth reminding ourselves that . . . pessimism
has not infrequently followed hard upon similar periods of
human progress. Thus in the era of greatest achievement
in the history of the Hebrew people, following the success-
ful wars of David and the national prestige gained under
Solomon, we find the stark pessimism of the book of Ec-
clesiastes closely associated with the magnificent spiritual
optimism of The Psalms. Like so many of our present day
scholars, the 'Preacher' could see little hope for permanent human progress." [28]

Salvation, for Miller, is an essentially human achievement.
Though he realizes that "radios and automobiles can be
passed down from one generation to another, [while] Euclid
and the Parable of the Good Samaritan must be painfully
parsed by each individual in the secret of his own chamber," [29]
Miller looks for cumulative moral growth.

"Who can say . . . that man's moral stature has not
been progressing through nineteen centuries of Christian
progress and may not still grow to the point where he can
cope successfully with the problems of a complex modern
society?" [30]

In this regard Miller conceives of a lag between material
progress (whose engine is purring smoothly) and the moral
forces of society (which are missing fire noticeably).[31]
He grants that "the biological heritage of self-interest as
it honeycombs the body politic . . . constitutes the major
threat to society." [32] But he proposes no radical step for overcoming this evil; rather, a moral force based upon man's
desire for social salvation.

Immortality in this picture is clearly corporate. A man's

" life is very truly built into the structure of human society." [33] If his contribution to life is good, it becomes part of the treasures of mankind; whereas, rust and moth will corrupt an evil contribution. Miller is not ready, however, to regard corporate or social immortality as the only possible alternative. He is a theistic humanist and combines it with more traditionally Christian elements. Thus, we find him saying, after affirming social immortality:

" Recognition of the immortality of man as he builds himself into society does not preclude the possibility that the mysterious core of his personality, having served in this life as a channel for mediating God's bounty to others, may yet be redeployed for future tasks. Having been ' faithful over a few things,' who is to say that he may not one day be ' ruler over many things '? " [34]

Most of the scientists we have discussed so far have been ethical idealists. For them the ethical life consists of following the dictates of high ideals, of doing the obvious good rather than a dubious evil. Miller breaks with this outlook, developing an ethical pragmatism, which he states as follows:

" Not merely may practices which exhibit no antisocial characteristics in a primitive society develop potentialities of evil in a more complex social organization; individuals may also be required in an imperfect society to engage in enterprises which run counter to the dictates of a sensitively attuned moral consciousness. Thus war, with its obvious violation of the sanctity of human life, may be an inescapable necessity for correcting evils present in the body politic, and may eventuate in the ultimate good of society." [35]

This willingness of Miller to regard the justification of an act as determinable only within its social context saves him from doctrinaire political theories of both the extreme right and the extreme left. He would seek " a balance between the forces tending to equalize opportunity and those seeking to promote progress by inequality." He does not find government evil per se and sees no ideological reason why it must stay out of social planning. He notes that

> " a small primitive group in society may be expected to function satisfactorily under the personal direction of just and capable leaders, but the huge social structures of modern times must be organized with a view toward as large a measure of automatic control as possible. This is no new discovery. The idea of a planned society, though anathema to many people, has dominated the hopes of mankind since the days of Moses and Plato." [36]

Pragmatism is not opportunism; Miller never lets go of an ideal standard. He recognizes the necessity of political action, both in peace and in war, but does not take this to imply that such action is merely a rough-and-tumble in which the strong man takes the spoils. He has a strong belief in democracy as the ability of a group to restrain the corruptions that threaten it from within as well as from without. Such a democracy can exist only if impregnated with " the vision of righteousness, justice, and altruism." " Let this vision," he says, " grow dim in a democratic society, as it did in ancient Rome, and the democratic ideal becomes a mockery and a delusion." [37]

The liberal Christian theists discussed in these chapters have all recognized the status of man as a child of God. In some of the thinkers this has led to an emphasis upon the human aspects of religion — a tendency most explicit in the discussion of this chapter. In proportion as Christian theism emphasizes the role of man, it may neglect the significance of God. When belief in God is vindicated on the supposed grounds of its constructive effect upon human behavior, does not God become secondary rather than primary, a construct of man rather than a constraint over him? If belief in God is a useful hypothesis, beneficial to human life, is not God man's creation rather than his Creator, dependent upon man's judgment rather than a judge over man?

Indeed, even in its own right, is not such an approach a flimsy basis for faith in God? Belief in God is not always beneficial to human life. Falsely used, it may become an escape from reality or a justification for a dogmatic arrogance that destroys the very fiber of human community. Surely, if belief in God hangs or falls on its social consequences, there are only meager grounds to justify it.

Theistic humanism maintains a very thin line between itself and its nontheistic brother. This comes not alone from its difficulty in maintaining an adequate conception of God but also from its very methodology of religion. By making an analogy, or identity, between science and religion based upon science as the prototype, it makes the subject matter of religion increasingly natural rather than supernatural, or, to use terms less freely tossed to and fro in contemporary debate, measurable and discoverable rather than immeasurable and self-revelatory.

The thin line involved here can be illustrated by two other figures. Edwin Grant Conklin, Princeton University biologist, develops a humanism on the basis of the evolutionary principle. In 1923 he signed the *Joint Statement Upon the Relation of Science and Religion* mentioned above, but his later writings move increasingly to a denial of the supernatural in religion. In 1943 he came to the conclusion that we can only be sure that man alone embodies purpose and plan in the universe, though we cannot prove that the universe is ruled by chance any more than we can prove that it is ruled by purpose.[38] By concentrating upon man, Conklin moves to an agnosticism about God. Likewise, Donald Dooley, Hiram College physics professor, writing an essay in W. E. Garrison's volume *Faith of the Free,* seeks a religion based on experiment and " as intelligent as science." [39] He asks that religion shed its supernatural features as the price of equality with scientific endeavor. He, like Conklin, stands on the line at which theism moves to nontheism. We have discussed their scientific colleagues on the expressly Christian side of this line; we turn now to those on the other side. This is a basic philosophical shift; it leaves the realm of more traditionally religious concepts, but it does not leave the realm of credos. Indeed it comes to an important and significant group of them — those with a secular outlook on life often claiming a unique allegiance to science and greatly influencing the thinking of the modern world.

V

NONTHEISTIC OUTLOOKS

*" The race will not save itself until it achieves intellectual morale.
. . . The two chief components of intellectual morale are intellectual integrity and a fierce conviction that man can become the master of his fate."* [1]
" A serious application of intelligence to the solution of social problems is worth attempting. I shall pause only long enough to remark that I would challenge the validity of the evidence on which the bellicose base their confidence in the efficacy of supernatural methods, and to point out to the apathetic despairers that the method of intelligence has never had a fair trial." [2]
— Percy W. Bridgman.

CONTEMPORARY philosophies of life that deny the existence of God are generally variations of naturalistic humanism, logical positivism, or atheistic existentialism. For natural scientists existentialism has little appeal, since it not only denies the reality of God but gives little positive impetus to the scientific enterprise. Consequently, the nontheistic outlooks of natural scientists fall into the first two categories.

While sharp differences exist between humanism and positivism regarding the applicability of the scientific method to the discovery of spiritual values, they nevertheless agree with each other in their rejection of the supernatural elements in religion and their common distrust of traditional religious authority. They share a basic conviction regarding the capacity of human intelligence, and it alone, to solve social problems and lead to the tolerably good society. They extol the scientific spirit as a prototype for that freedom of inquiry and openness of mind upon which they feel democratic society ultimately depends.

The line between theistic and nontheistic humanism is not absolute. In fact, when one discovers a Christian such as Kirtley Mather, of Harvard, writing in the volumes of the Conference on Scientific Spirit and the Democratic Faith, he wonders if there is any line at all. At least he is warned against pigeonholing individuals by the company they keep or trying to judge the content of a scientist's thought by identifying him as a member of a particular philosophical school.

Nontheistic humanism need not blurt out, " The idea of God is the wishful thinking of a prescientific age "; it need only make the question of God a purely optional or peripheral one by occupying itself solely with empirical and human categories. By emphasis upon the natural and by omission of the divine, even more than by categorical rejection of theistic doctrines, it can imply that man faces life alone; that is, without supernatural aid or comfort. Even so, it constitutes an outlook that is religious in character.

Consider Vannevar Bush's best-selling work, *Modern Arms and Free Men.*[3] Granted it discusses the problem of maintaining a democratic bulwark in a threatening world, this book is like a credo in that it reveals again and again an underlying faith.

We find no specific commitment to any traditional religious outlook in Bush's book — it contains no mention of God. Probably Bush feels no need to commit himself at this point, and perhaps even a wisdom in not doing so. He seeks a line-up of liberal forces against the totalitarian forces threatening democracy, and, for the purposes of his book, might even feel that a discussion of religious metaphysics would destroy the unity he seeks.

Bush's basic category is democratic freedom: " The world is split into two camps. In blunt summary terms, there are on the one hand those who believe in freedom and the dignity of man and on the other hand those who believe in a supreme conquering state to which all men would be slaves." [4] A great company of men of good will believe in human freedom, and they stand united against its enemies.

" It is a varied company, for it includes those who adhere to the great formal religions, those who do not thus adhere but who have faith, and those who order their lives apart from deep religious thinking but who have hope for man and believe he is capable of building a better world." [5]

Bush is pluralistic. The crucial line-up of men who favor democracy and freedom and oppose political totalitarianism and applied materialism (which is Bush's terminology for Russian political Communism) can include both adherents of formal religions and men without fixed creeds. The key mark is belief in freedom.

" The company believes in freedom; it believes passionately in freedom of the individual. Instinctively if you will, and quite apart from its logical analysis of how man came to his present state, it believes that there is something in the free creativeness of individuals that is worth preserving in the world." [6]

Bush would probably disagree with those adherents of the scientific spirit who strongly attack traditional religious categories. He explicitly denies that science teaches a harsh materialism. " It does not teach anything at all beyond its boundaries, and those boundaries are severely limited by science itself." [7] Science deals with the sensible, and some things " are forever beyond its ken." It does not, for example, tell whether or not there was a great purpose at work in creation. It does not answer the question, " Why? " in any final or ultimate sense. It does not answer the question as to whether man is a product of chance or plan, or whether he is determined or free.

Bush is vehement against those who draw the conclusion from science that "mankind is engaged merely in a futile dance, a meaningless fluttering over the cruel surface of the earth before an inexorable curtain descends, with no more to life than a struggle for a seamy existence." [8] These thinkers, as Bush sees it, arrive at such conclusions by a fallacy — the fallacy of dogmatizing that sense perception encompasses all there is to reality. This, indeed, has been used by many as evidence that Bush strongly attacks the naturalists. This does not follow. He is perhaps casting some slander at a type of positivism that includes no real constructive attitude toward man (a very rare form of it) and at a type of existentialism that wants to grit its teeth blindly against a hostile nature. Bush himself specifically identifies the materialistic thinkers as those who have produced the Russian threat. " From such a fallacy come materialism and the new fatalism now built into a political system geared for conquest." [9]

The company of freedom on which Bush pins the hopes of democracy " believes in the dignity of man, and shows this in its actions. While it is perfectly willing to admit that man has made a sorry spectacle of himself, and that his way can be disgusting as no beast ever disgusts, yet it is not willing to describe all of man's actions solely in terms of selfishness, or weakness, or depravity." [10]

Thus Bush's book is flavored with Dewey's " common faith," a pluralistic willingness to join with all men of good will in strengthening the noble aspects of humanity in a democratic culture. To this, however, Bush adds a quite new twist and one that reflects the crisis of the years within which he writes. Democracy is worth preserving for its intrinsic value; about this Bush is certain and eloquent. But it is also vindicated, or, perhaps, more exactly, preserved, by its ability to keep ahead in a world of conflict and of power.

Freedom of research and the interchange of ideas that occur in the open nature of public scientific work as fostered by a democracy — these will guarantee freedom. Freedom springs both from (1) internal idealism and (2) external vigilance and strength. " Modern arms " is a symbolic term for the second element. Bush counts on winning a power struggle against the forces of antifreedom. He minces no words as to the cost of the enterprise and evidences little moral reservation about the use of every scientific weapon of destruction needed to defeat a wartime enemy. Bush knows he is painting prospects of a type of warfare not pleasant to contemplate. But, almost in a strain of thought that one might characterize as existentialist, he notes that this is the price of freedom. This is the way it is, and we must meet it. Bush remains a cool and apparently dispassionate observer in all his discussion of the weapons of modern war — weapons and methods that make Buck Rogers' adventures look like child's play.

In two chapters dealing with the more specific functions by which a democracy keeps itself strong, Bush repeats the general attitudes that form symbols of usual pragmatic humanist thought. He has strong faith in an education that is scientific and pragmatic in its basic aim. He favors the National Science Foundation, which by implication is to favor a utilitarian concern in education, in contrast, say, to a " great books " philosophy of learning. Then, too, while he is wary of too much governmental planning, he deals with the issue pragmatically, not doctrinarily as some of those who cry for " free " enterprise. He would measure planning by results, and while he predicts that results will come from a yearning for a minimum rather than a maximum of governmental interference, this balance is to be guided, not merely left to chance.

We have placed Vannevar Bush in this Chapter, not be-cause he has specifically committed himself to a definite at-titude on the matter of religion — he has done quite the reverse and avoided a specific stand — but because the moti-vating urges out of which Bush writes are characteristic of a humanism with a democratic faith. That Bush has not specif-ically committed himself on religious issues and that he gives large and tolerant place to wide variations in religious out-looks (provided they join the company that believes in free-dom) suggests that Bush is pluralistic in his underlying attitudes. Also in this scheme freedom becomes the ulti-mately important category. Pluralism is a form of humanism; those who seriously believe in God cannot make the question of his existence peripheral.

Percy W. Bridgman, whose quotation heads this chapter, comes closer to a standard type of nontheistic humanism. His belief in democracy and humanism includes more philosoph-ical formulation and evidences less patience with a super-naturalism. Bush left room for traditional religious ideas be-yond the ken of science; Bridgman writes:

" The man in the street will, therefore, twist the state-ment that the scientist has come to the end of meaning into the statement that the scientist has penetrated as far as he can with the tools at his command, and that there is something beyond the ken of the scientist. This imagined beyond, which the scientist has proved he cannot pene-trate, will become the playground of the imagination of every mystic and dreamer. The existence of such a domain will be made the basis of an orgy of rationalizing. It will be made the substance of the soul; the spirits of the dead will populate it; God will lurk in its shadows; the principle of vital processes will have its seat here; and it will be the medium of telepathic communication. One group will find in the failure of the physical law of cause and effect the solution of the agelong problem of the freedom of the will; and on the other hand the atheist will find the justification of his contention that chances rule the universe." [11]

Bridgman's opposition to supernaturalism also appears in his criticism of a society that does not seek to contact him as an understanding man, "but tries to get hold of me by absolutes and supernaturals and verbalism." [12] But, except in these remarks and a few like them, Bridgman is concerned to state his own constructive suggestions, rather than merely to attack religion. Perhaps he believes that the case against traditional religious understanding has been made so convincing by the philosophers that he himself need not refight the battle.

It is not the function of this treatment to expound Bridgman's philosophy of science beyond that point necessary to understand his *Weltanschauung*. Bridgman has furnished a new and powerful concept to the epistemology of science — the concept of operational meaning. In it meaning and truth are measured by reproducibility in activity — by an operation. Facts are directions for action, and Bridgman is highly skeptical of those facts (mainly value judgments and ideals) which cannot meet the operational test.

Another contribution of Bridgman is his emphasis upon the individuality of knowledge. He does not mean this, of course, in the sense of permitting every man the free run of the imagination, but rather in the sense that knowledge must be individually appropriated and accepted. Thus he suggests "that science is essentially private, whereas, the almost universal counter point of view, explicitly stated in many of the articles of the Encyclopedia, is that it *must* be public." [13] For Bridgman, to say, "I understand," is to make a statement as equally private in character as to say, " My tooth aches." Unless one understands privately, he doesn't understand at all — regardless of any confessions to the contrary made in expediency or " to silence too vociferous an instructor." When science is public, as it should be, it is public only in so far as there is agreement as to private understandings.

This " individualism " of Bridgman naturally and logically involves an individualism in ethics and social outlook:

" Three stages of evolution can be recognized in the present philosophy of the relation of the individual to society. The first granted the right of the bright people to exploit the stupid ones; the second recognized the right of everyone to receive from society a reward proportional to his contribution to society; and the third and present stage recognizes the right of the stupid people to exploit the bright ones. It is perhaps obvious that my sympathies are with the second, or median of these three philosophies." [14] Bridgman pushes this ethical individualism to all its practical consequences. He suggests that our democracy is growing sentimental because it glorifies the common man — who is also the mediocre man. He suggests, " The [Marxist] slogan, ' to everybody according to his need, from everybody according to his abilities ' . . . is not generally regarded as admirable or consistent with self-respect in this country, but this is exactly what is involved in the philosophy which justifies our graded income tax." [15] He proposes a return to the concept of minimum governmental control to put a stop to the taking of money from some to give it to others. He is critical of a totalitarian society that demands absolute allegiance to the will of the majority. He is also critical of a conventional Christian society " with its thesis that the good life is the one devoted to the service of a man's fellows, and with the correlative assumption of the right of the community to impose this ideal on the individual." [16]

Bridgman deals with the limitations of science in a way that leads naturally to logical positivism. He is not a consistent positivist who carries the emphasis on sense perception to an inexorable conclusion that denies all other truth. But he does hesitate to speculate concerning the area beyond the ken of science.

" The world is not intrinsically reasonable or understandable; it acquires these properties in ever-increasing degree as we ascend from the realm of the very little to the realm of everyday things; here we may eventually hope for an understanding sufficiently good for all practical purposes, but no more." [17]

"We had thought the human reason capable of conquering all things, we now find it subject to very definite limitations. We can definitely conjure up physical situations in which the human reason is powerless to satisfy itself, but must passively be content to accept phenomena as they occur, which constitutes in fact a reversion to the mental attitude of primitive man, which is purely receptive." [18]

When the physicist finds that the bottom has dropped out of his world — that is in quanta " where knowledge must stop because of the nature of knowledge itself " — the world eludes the physicist in the " highly unsportsmanlike device of just becoming meaningless." [19]

Philipp Frank, the Harvard physicist and admirer of Albert Einstein, is representative of a group that carries Bridgman's thought into a more logical denial of truth developed apart from sense perception. He is a member of the group, composed mostly of philosophers of science rather than natural scientists, working on the *International Encyclopedia of Unified Science,* and holding, in the main, a positivistic view of science and knowledge.

Positivism is not a religious creed, particularly in its own eyes, but it is an attitude toward life and toward the matters commonly dealt with in religious thought that is a live option among competing philosophical allegiances. It is negatively religious, strongly convinced of its task to disavow ontological, metaphysical, and theological speculation.

Frank's 1941 book, *Between Physics and Philosophy*,[20] is a strong and careful statement of the position that "spiritual" values are not to be found (negatively or positively) in science. It contains sharp criticism of many of the attempts, both American and British, to find theological significance in the thought revolution of modern physics. Frank asserts with some vehemence that relativity does not reinforce "subjectivism," nor quanta mechanics, a teleological outlook.[21] The real revolution in physics is a shift from reducing everything to mechanics to reducing everything to mathematics. In this early book Frank is concerned with epistemology, with the negative task of denying that metaphysical implications can be drawn from scientific truths. But in a 1950 book, *Relativity: a Richer Truth*,[22] he develops ethical and moral attitudes that, if not drawn from the scientific aspects of modern physics, are at least pictured as analogous to them.

Frank is critical of the physicist who gives his allegiance to schools of popular philosophy. He regards this as producing nothing but ambiguous expressions and placing the blessing of science upon existing confusion. Physicists who misuse the Heisenberg principle are seeking a bigger audience than strictly scientific activity brings them and thereby emulate the preacher. He suggests that for science the distinction between a "spiritualistic" *Weltanschauung* and a "materialistic" one is unessential, especially when the same observable facts follow from one as from another. "What matters, to repeat the words of William James, is the 'cash value' of a set of principles." [23]

This being true, Frank then makes the interesting observation that follows:

"If you sympathize with the ethical goal of a religious group, you will easily agree with its way of speaking. The scientist who is strongly aware of the wide margin within which he can choose his language will be willing to use the language of the group with which he is politically or ethically in sympathy. I do not mean to denounce this way of conduct as cheap opportunism. It is natural behavior in the delicate terrain of scientific and ethical discourse. But it certainly has nothing to do with the integration of our knowledge by a universal philosophy." [24]

Frank may be suggesting a "unified ethic" — an attempt to find ethical agreement and understanding among many different religious groups by clipping off excess metaphysical baggage. Such an attempt emphasizes that the drives of logical positivism can be constructive and, incidentally, of close kinship with the pluralism of nontheistic humanism. Frank's concept of "ethical cash value" might be a humanistic proposal for getting the real meat of all religious ethics from off the theological bones.

In this regard he comments upon the thought of Albert Einstein. Frank interprets Einstein's thought in his own way and makes the following observation:

"This historical experience of 'rationality' is undeniable. It may be debatable whether we must see in this fact the result of a 'divine' plan or whether such an assumption would lead us into the dangerous waters of anthropomorphism. The fact of the 'rationality of nature' is independent of all interpretations which have been traditionally called 'purposiveness of nature.' The belief in this rationality is what Einstein has called *cosmic religion*. It is a belief in a certain correlation between nature and the human mind. The correlation has been described for hundreds and thousands of years by saying that the world has been created by a mind which has some properties of the human mind although it is much superior. This is the language of traditional religion organized in churches or of individual faith. Whether one keeps to this 'religious' way of speaking depends upon whether one believes that there are human values in the work of the organized groups who have used this language. If we sympathize with the human values in the work of such groups, we shall be inclined to describe this cosmic religion by using such traditionally venerable words as ' God '; but if we believe that the tradition has degenerated and that its present heirs do not strive for satisfactory human goals, then we may accentuate our disapproval by departing from the orthodox language of these groups.

"Einstein has been convinced that there are immense human values in the Judaeo-Christian tradition and used freely the word ' God ' in referring to his cosmic religion." [25]

Frank's ethical thought is an application of the principle of relativity to the problems of human action. He is sharply critical of idealistic philosophy, which he accuses of favoring, and being favored by, totalitarianism. Idealistic philosophy, as Frank sees it, "facilitates the conception that principles that appear correct can and must be carried out, regardless of the fate they determine for human beings." [26] On the other hand, a pragmatic ethic (relativity in its ethical form) judges action solely by concrete consequences in particular situations. Also "when the most vigorous ethical principles [are] applied in special cases, their guidance [does] not differ much from that which results from mere opportunism and adjustment to local prejudices." [27] Hence, Frank levels a twofold criticism at idealistic ethics. First, they operate ideologically rather than with concern for concrete considerations; secondly, in so far as they express themselves historically they tend to be opportunistic.

Science and the scientific spirit pay particular concern to concrete results, and therefore have much in common with pragmatic ethics. Thus, science, as a great body of ideas subject to constant revision, and the scientific spirit, as the willingness to change them, are bulwarks of democracy against totalitarianism. This scientific spirit is evident among the pure scientists, the physicists, and mathematicians, but ". . . the percentage of convinced nationalists and chauvinists . . . is notably large among students of those fields devoted to the practical application of . . . sciences. I have encountered the most uncritical of all the adherents of totalitarianism among the students of, for example, engineering." [28]

Sophisticated philosophies that deny the meaning of metaphysical and religious speculation have an unsophisticated counterpart. This unsophisticated counterpart — which, because of its very character, is not set down in written credos — is a philosophy held by men who regard the type of problems discussed above as so much idle chatter. Such homespun agnostics are not interested in the issues involved in an intelligent and thoughtful religious world view and can merely be mentioned in a book that analyzes more carefully reasoned credos. This agnosticism is certainly no more characteristic of men of natural science than any of the other views considered here. While prevalent, it is by no means normative.

In the material to date we have discussed specific philosophical attitudes that consciously and clearly seek to develop a sound religious faith by looking at the scientific picture of the world. Another attitude remains to be discussed; perhaps it is more an enthusiasm than a religious philosophy. It is a religious phenomenon springing out of full allegiance to a scientific way of life and giving written expression to its feeling. It has its philosophical categories and its ethical ideals, but it is to be primarily understood as a zestful following of science as a way of life and a pseudo worship of all that it can do for humankind. We have chosen to call it " enthusiasm for science and invention."

VI

ENTHUSIASM FOR SCIENCE AND INVENTION

"You have heard a great deal about science, research and engineering. But for every experiment that has been a success, there have been thousands of failures, much discouragement and sleepless nights. Long hours have been spent in just thinking about and experimenting with these developments. If that work had not been done, man would not be flying. We would have no electric lights, no motorcars, nor could you now be listening to this great orchestra.
"So the thing that really started and maintains progress in the world is man's ability to think, and his dissatisfaction with things as they are. That is the intangible motive power *which makes for human progress."* [1]
"There will always be a frontier where there is an open mind and a willing hand." [2] — Charles F. Kettering.

THE activity of research and discovery can become an all-consuming passion. It can become an object of enthusiasm and devotion, even though it may carry with it no specifically doctrinal religious creed and no particular philosophical speculation. This enthusiasm may give itself expression in spoken and written discourse, and when it does, it becomes a " religious " type of thought.

It would be unfair to suggest that this attitude engages in specific polemics against other creeds, or even that an enthusiasm of this sort is necessarily divorced from one or another of the religious and philosophical orientations discussed above. A theist can have enthusiasm for the scientific enterprise as well as a nontheist, and either can give it wide-spread expression without once committing himself on metaphysical issues. Nevertheless, certain scientists write about the scientific enterprise as a great adventure; they represent a particular approach with a flavor all its own.

Arthur Compton, whom we have met elsewhere and who belongs elsewhere because of the many things he has to say about God, sometimes gives expression to this enthusiasm for science. It falls to his brother, Karl Taylor Compton, however, to illustrate this chapter. His writings tell us very little about Karl Compton's formal religious outlook. Instead, we find in them a continuous emphasis upon the tremendous significance of science for our modern culture and a constant desire to make the reader aware of how rich a blessing is scientific achievement. He suggests that science has changed pioneering from the earlier, "Go west, young man, go west!" to a dedication of the self to science and invention.

He praises science for the tremendous opportunities it offers for the creation of new gadgets.[3] He is eager to point out that science is the creative factor in modern civilization. He entitles an address to the Modern Pioneers Association "Science, the Soul of Prosperity." In it he suggests that science makes possible the creation of wealth, not mere competition for it; it thus furnishes the prospect for overcoming economic injustice in a free economy (without the imposition of governmental controls). This capacity of science to create new riches has its international implications too:

"By creating wealth and opportunity where they did not exist before, the engineer has struck a mighty blow against the primitive predatory instinct that breeds so much trouble between nations and between classes within nations."[4]

In an address delivered at Rutgers in 1942 he reaffirms his

enthusiasm for scientific activity. Recognizing the shadow of the Second World War and treating the relationship of science to it as a temporary side trip made for the sake of preserving American freedom, he goes on:

"One can certainly say that the scientists should face the year 1942 with enthusiasm and confidence in the possibilities of new achievement. Far from feeling that the age of scientific discovery is past because all presently known scientific discoveries have already been made, the informed faith of the true scientist is that the opportunities which now lie ahead are greater than those possessed by any previous generation of scientists in the history of the world." [5]

That the scientific enterprise so rapidly achieves its results and produces such thrilling outcomes, that progress in science is so rapid and certain, is attributed by Compton to two factors: (1) the devotion of an increasing number of young men and women with scientific ambition and training, aided in their careers by educational and philanthropic organizations, and (2) the constant acceleration that takes place in scientific activity as greater and greater knowledge is added to the rapidly growing body of scientific information.

Even more basic than either of these is the factor of political freedom. Science cannot function well except under freedom — a theme about which Compton speaks his mind as firmly and eloquently as Bush:

"It is certainly more than a coincidence that the age of great scientific progress has coincided exactly with the age in which individuals have had freedom of thought and action and personal initiative." [6]

Because of this, Compton feels that the scientists had a tremendous stake in the outcome of the struggle for freedom as represented by World War II, and in current utterances gives vent to the same conviction about the East-West conflict.

These firm convictions of Compton about the great significance of science and the interrelatedness of the destiny of science with that of democratic freedom are sprinkled liberally throughout all his writings. These writings are themselves dedicated to the carrying forward of the scientific task, to the integrating and unifying of all research workers into a common brotherhood, and to the making of scientific research an all-important cog in the life and economy of American civilization. Compton is a statesman of scientific endeavor.

Another representative of this approach and concern, writing for a less professional group than Compton and spelling out somewhat more fully some of the driving urges and enthusiasms behind his task, is Charles F. Kettering. The character of his writing is probably dictated by its use as intermission talks for the General Motors program, "The Symphony of the Air." These have been collected and printed by the General Motors Corporation in a booklet entitled, *Short Stories of Science and Invention.* This is a popular presentation of the romantic stories behind many scientific developments. It is simple and direct, but nevertheless permeated with an outlook and attitude toward science that contains a pseudoreligious element. Kettering stresses, in the first place, the tremendous significance of technical science, both as a way of life for the scientist and as a source of blessing for civilization. Science is a frontier, an ever open way of opportunity, for those who are ready and willing to work with mind and hands. The opportunities that come by, and through, invention are endless and offer promise of a great future. "What is known of nature's processes is very little indeed and the World of Today will seem quite primitive and amateurish in the light of discoveries to be made in the World of Tomorrow." [7]

The frontier of science, as Kettering romanticizes it, is not only unlimited, but noble and grand. In contrast with the four horsemen of the Apocalypse — War, Famine, Pestilence, and Death — the four horsemen of Peace are Hope, Experience, Good Sense, and Science.[8] Of these, the horseman of Science leads the way — the way of new discovery, of limitless horizons, of useful discoveries fairly begging to be uncovered. With this promise, even though peaceful pursuit aggregates more slowly than wartime destructiveness, tomorrow will become a great new era in civilization's onward march.

Obstacles to this onward march can appear only from within men themselves, or, conversely speaking, opportunity is within the individual. There is "no fairy godmother pointing out the Road to Success." Rather, success comes where

"there is the *desire* and *ability* to create — to do something original — something *no one* has ever done or been able to do before. Second, there is the quality of *persistence*, the urge to keep going until it is finished — regardless of surroundings, poverty or health. Third, there is that *dissatisfaction* which seems to be the standard equipment of these men. Regardless of how outstanding their work appears to the world, they themselves are never satisfied with it and are sure if they had it to do over again they could have done a better job." [9]

In this type of attitude we find a great emphasis upon individual ability and ambition, upon patience in doing a job and persistence in face of difficulty. But these are always assumed by Kettering to be of an individual character, possessed by the single scientist at work alone in his laboratory. Nowhere in his book does Kettering strongly emphasize the co-operative nature of research or adequately portray the mutual search for discovery that characterizes the modern scientific enterprise. This is strange, for Kettering headed the research work of the General Motors Corporation, and surely he did not administer his complex responsibilities in terms of individual endeavor, the prototype of scientific research he uses for his radio talks. At this point Karl Compton, who recognizes the fraternal and corporate nature of research and discovery and clearly portrays the scientific enterprise in terms that point it out, is a much clearer and wiser guide.

Kettering joins the majority of scientists favoring freedom of scientific research and opposing governmentally planned and controlled investigation. However, he makes more explicit what is sometimes implicit in other apologists for freedom, for he indicates the close affinity he believes necessary between science and business. It is on the level of business that teamwork appears.

" Every phase of our modern civilization owes much to the hard work and teamwork of several groups of men. First to those who invent, second to those who provide and risk money on what appears at the time to be a foolish idea, third to the skilled craftsmen who help build the devices — and fourth to the managerial ability of those who know how to put them into practical form, thereby making them available to the public and, at the same time, providing jobs for thousands of people." [10]

The ability to think forms the intangible in human progress. This ability is the " thing that really started and maintains progress." [11] The idea is the intangible seed of new discovery. But, this must be severely qualified, for ideas alone do no good. It is useless just to sit and philosophize, for only by the cut-and-try method of groping in the dark and testing every hunch can technical progress be brought about.

Much of what Kettering suggests is dated not so much perhaps by the time of its appearance (during World War II) but by its social outlook and its individualistic assumptions concerning the nature of the scientific task. Even when Kettering recognizes the teamwork between business and science, he does so in a way that condones a strong individualism in both. There is no suggestion whatsoever of the role of the Government in co-ordinating, directing, or financing scientific enterprise, no idea of a Manhattan project or its possibilities.

In so far as enthusiasm for science and invention becomes an all-consuming passion, the source of life's meaning for any individual, it must, from the Christian point of view, be regarded as an idolatry. It has probably not reached these proportions in either Compton's or Kettering's thinking; we have no grounds for believing that theirs is other than a justified zeal for vocational endeavor. It is unfortunate, however, that in giving vent to their zeal both these men divorce the secular from the religious. How much more meaningful would be an enthusiasm for science and invention that grounded itself in the doctrine of divine vocation — the service of God in a secular calling! It is a commentary on the age for which these men have written that they have seen fit to extol the scientific enterprise without relation to the religious dimension, which finally encompasses all quests for truth.

We have moved a long way from Einstein to Kettering — a way of great diversity of outlook with many different types of thought. However, one common thread runs throughout: all the scientists we have discussed so far are basically trying to move from science to religion. They are seeking to answer the question, " What in science lends support to religion, and what kind of religion is thus supported? " In some cases this is explicitly asked; in other cases it is only implicit, even deeply buried.

To be sure, the form of the question may vary. Perhaps it asks, " What in science itself is religious in character? " Or again, " What in science points to another reality that can be called religious? " Or again, " What in science shows us that we can know very little about any reality (if there is any) beyond the realm of sense data? " All these questions contrast themselves with another set. This second set asks more typically: " How can science fit such and such a religious outlook? " " How can the facts of science be reconciled with such and such a conception of the ultimate character of the cosmos? " Questions of this second type move basically from religion to science and underlie the types of thought in the coming section. In it we discuss philosophies in which the religious presupposition overshadows the scientific one, in which religion is given first allegiance; science, second.

In a scientific age, or more exactly, in an age in which the prestige of science is strong and the desire to be " scientific " the all-consuming passion, the first type of approach is more popular than the second. In this first section are the scientists who are the popular exponents of the compatibility of science and religious faith; they are the men who use the categories of modern philosophic verbiage.

Difficulties in developing a religious creed from arguments based on scientific knowledge become all too apparent in the examination of even the most sophisticated and adequate attempts. The diversity and disagreement encountered among scientists supposedly basing their credos upon scientific considerations makes one wonder how much relevance science has to religion. That the scientists do not draw similar religious conclusions from similar scientific considerations would lend a provisional support to the religious temperament that is all too prone to dismiss without examination the possible relevance of science to religious truth. About this issue, however, we shall be wiser to maintain a reserved judgment until the evidence of the coming section is examined. Here religious truth is loyal only to itself, and at times even seeks to dictate to scientific outlooks. The potential fruitfulness of this type of approach bears scrutiny on the same basis as that of philosophies already studied. It is with this thought in mind that we move to the next part, examining philosophies loyal first to a religious system and second (if at all) to scientific truth.

PART TWO

APPROACHES THROUGH RELIGION

VII

BIBLICAL STATEMENT AND SCIENTIFIC FACT:

CREATIONISM

*" In building his philosophy the special creationist begins with
the few basic facts regarding biological beginning and continu-
ance which are found in the Bible. However, because of the
paucity of information from this source he is largely dependent
upon facts in the natural world for the superstructure of his philosophy. When the interpretation of material from the natural
world is truthful and when the phenomenon is mentioned in the
Bible, he finds harmony between it and the Bible record."* [1]
— Frank Lewis Marsh.

CHAPTER IV discussed the thought of certain men who
find the theory of evolution a true and adequate description of natural growth. It noted their attempts to relate
a religious outlook to this scientific hypothesis. Now we come
to a group of men whose persuasion on the matter of evolution is quite the opposite. They question the theory and affirm a doctrine of creation. They are of interest here because
a particular religious orientation lies behind their thought.
It is to their creedal position that our major interest will be
directed.

E. Ralph Hooper, for twenty-one years demonstrator in the
Anatomical Department of the Medical Faculty of the University of Toronto, in a little book asking *Does Science Support Evolution?* answers his question negatively. In doing so,
he openly declares Biblicistic presuppositions. In a section

entitled "Testimony," Hooper relates how courses in science caused his faith to slip. He goes on to point out that his questionings were overcome, not by sophisticated theological argument, but by a literal interpretation of the Bible. He caustically criticizes the divinity faculty of his college for offering him no help and tells how, under fundamentalist tutelage,

"The Holy Spirit revealed the Bible to me as being the Word of God. All doubts vanished. A sense of rest and assurance filled my soul. I now knew that my feet were planted on solid ground. The speculations, the assumptions, the self-assurance of these doubting and deluded critics now seemed to me to be the veriest trifles. On the other hand, God now became authoritative, majestic. His Word became to me final and its foundation the bedrock of truth." [2]

Hooper's entire work is permeated by a desire to vindicate the Biblical doctrine of creation. He maintains, however, that science itself is the court of appeal. "Evolution has taken issue with the Bible account of Creation, as recorded in Genesis. Science will be found to support either the one or the other; to science then we shall appeal." [3]

Hooper is able to suggest this framework for the inquiry because he sharply distinguishes between "science" and "evolution." The one is a knowledge of facts, laws, and proximate causes; the other is imagination — speculation without foundation. Thus evolution (which is imagination) and creation (which is inspiration) are mutually contradictory — and one or the other must be discredited. These are contending views in a death struggle with each other; there can be no compromise between them. Hooper has no conception of a possible resolution between the one as scientific fact and the other as religious evaluation, no idea of a dialectical unity worked out between the two. Despite his claims to the contrary, Hooper is not leaving the issue scientifically open. If he were — granting his analysis that the Bible hangs or falls as evolution hangs or falls as a scientific theory — he would be putting his religion at the mercy of a scientific theory, and this would most crucially undercut his authoritarian concept of Biblical truth.

What are the reasons that Hooper advances as scientific evidence for creationism as against an evolutionary doctrine? In the first place he makes capital of all admissions on the part of evolutionists, such as Henry Fairfield Osborn, that the theory is not completely watertight and that there are gaps in the experimental evidence. He suggests that because the exponents of evolution admit the theory is a hypothesis, it cannot be a scientific fact; since it is not a scientific fact, it is, therefore, wrong. The obvious problem of logic here is not apparent to Hooper, because he regards the Christian doctrine of creation as factual, therefore scientific, and clearly preferable to a " hypothesis."

In the second place Hooper emphasizes the biological evidence that " like produces like." Dogs do not produce cats; nor birds, elephants. Certain species represent irreducible categories. These species could not arise except by creation. They come into existence suddenly and in full perfection. Thus Hooper summarizes his case: " Evolution has failed to explain the existence of the material universe, [whereas] the Bible explains the existence of the universe with ' In the beginning God.' Evolution has failed to explain the origin of mechanical and chemical energy, [whereas] the Bible explains the origin of energy, ' Let there be light.' Evolution has failed to prove the spontaneous generation of life or that the one-celled protozoan is the originate of the many-celled animal, [whereas] the Bible explains the existence of Life, ' God created! ' Evolution has failed to prove the transmutation of species, to prove that any one species has fundamentally changed throughout the centuries of life, or to prove that one cell can produce cells different from itself in function, [whereas] the Bible explains the existence of separate and immutable species. 'God created . . . herbs . . . trees . . . birds . . . sea monsters . . . cattle . . . and creeping things and beasts.' Evolution has failed to bridge the gap between cold-blooded reptiles and warm-blooded animals, to produce one missing link between man and apes, or between any two distinct species, to explain the existence of some form of mentality in all animal life, or the existence of intelligence, rational power, and spiritual inclinations in man, [whereas] the Bible explains the immutability of species, each 'after his kind.' The Bible explains the origin of man as separate from the apes and from the lower animals, 'Let us make man in our image.' " [4]

The Biblicistic presuppositions in this type of argument are clearly apparent. Hooper could be taken more seriously in his discussion of the scientific issues if the religious categories were less blindly accepted. Hooper's book shows too much dependence upon the ideas of others; no really creative work is going on in his presentation. On the one hand, the quickness with which Hooper will pick out every flaw in the argument supporting evolution, and on the other hand, completely accept the presuppositions of literalism, is clue enough to the one-sidedness of his outlook.

The creationist position has been more responsibly stated by Frank Lewis Marsh, professor of biology at Union College in Lincoln, Nebraska. He presents the general arguments used by Hooper with considerably more sophistication. While Hooper relies largely on quotations from other scientists, used both in context and out of context, Marsh has an apparent command of his material, especially of the scientific issues involved.

Marsh starts his book, *Evolution, Creation and Science,* with the suggestion that evolution is accepted in scientific circles because of a professional pressure that fosters the doctrine with a cocksure zeal. Speaking of the training of young scientists, he notes, concerning their acceptance of evolution:

" The thing which repeatedly won them over to acceptance of the theory was sheer weight of authority on the part of scientists through a not always highly refined method of browbeating. All too frequently if the young aspirant was to keep face with the more seasoned scientists, he was obliged to accept the evolution theory." [5]

In this accusation Marsh is assuming that evolution is theory — and a theory that does not follow simply from factual data at hand. " When [a scientist] gives you a theory of origins he has ceased to be a scientist and has become a philosopher." [6]

Marsh's attack upon main-stream scientific opinion also complains that evolutionists are unfair to creationist thinking. He points to samplings from biology textbooks as proof that evolutionists are prone to caricature creationism. Typical of the suggestions Marsh ridicules is one in which an evolutionist author points out that if woman was made from a rib taken from man then we should expect man to have one less rib than woman. An evolutionist who chooses to attack creationism on this level deserves Marsh's ridicule. Usually we expect this level of attack from the other side, from obscurantists seeking to undermine a commonly accepted scientific outlook. Marsh admits this; he speaks thus of the total situation: " Many very unfair and inaccurate statements against evolution have been made by individuals, not scientists, who hold to a theory of special creation." [7]

In contrast to this antagonistic attitude between the two groups and zealous allegiance to theory despite facts, Marsh appeals for new scientific evaluation of the evidence. This, he feels, will support a doctrine of creation — at least it will show the impossibility of proving the theory of evolution.

"The doctrine of special creation is not merely a creed to be accepted by faith. It appeals to the spiritual faculties, and also to the logical. Every fact of natural science is explainable logically from the viewpoint of special creation. In actual practice less faith is necessary in its application to nature than in the acceptance of the theory of organic evolution." [8]

The scientific aspect of Marsh's case is based on the idea of "Genesis kinds." These are basic species, which change and growth can modify but not transcend. This is the idea that Hooper puts forth as "like produces like" and is pictured clearly in Marsh's own terms as follows:

"Cats forever remain cats, although varying from tabbies to lions; and dogs remain dogs, although changing from great Danes to poodles. The Drosophila with all his one thousand-plus mutations has never achieved anything other than a vinegar fly." [9]

Marsh places special emphasis upon the tremendous flexibility within each category. He does not clamp down a rigid dictum, "No change at all"; he gives a large place to the many changes that occur within each basic kind or species. This he feels is necessary to maintain truth and an adequate interpretation of the facts. He wants neither extreme — neither the one denying all change nor the one suggesting that change itself has produced all the variations of species.

It is the religious presuppositions of Marsh's thought in which we are primarily interested. Marsh, like Hooper, regards it as necessary for a satisfactory unity between science and Christianity that scientific facts and literally understood Biblical evidence be in essential agreement.

"The special creationist builds this theory from the statements in Genesis in conjunction with the facts in nature. One source complements the other. This union of Bible statement with all scientific facts enables the biologist to form a complete theory which includes the whole span of living things from their origin to the present moment." [10]

Marsh does not believe that he is asserting that the Bible is right despite what science says. He writes, rather, out of a faith that there will be no opposition between science and Genesis if both are properly understood. "When the interpretation of material from the natural world is truthful and when the phenomenon is mentioned in the Bible, [the special creationist] finds harmony between it and the Bible record." [11]

Marsh accepts the authority of the Bible; he feels that the Bible carries our knowledge of the natural world beyond what we can know by observation. While thus accepting the authority of Genesis, he goes on to make the interesting suggestion that "the briefness of the Genesis record of origins makes possible considerable variation in the finer details of the creeds of individuals who accept the theory of special creation." [12] Here Marsh is rejoicing in a freedom not usually associated with men sharing his view of inspiration.

Marsh's own creed includes belief in a creation completed as a unit in six days. "The record is that it was *finished,* and the seventh day was set apart as a special day to commemorate the *completion* of the creation of all organic forms." [13] It includes belief in the " Genesis kinds," basic species, which do not and cannot cross with each other even though they do undergo modification within themselves. It includes belief in a deluge as described in the flood accounts of Genesis. It includes belief in the Bible as having central authority in matters of faith and morals — holding to its authority in a direct and nondialectical fashion.

Marsh is ultimately concerned about salvation. " Christ did

not die to redeem a noble beast, but rather, to make possible
the reinstatement of the fallen members of God's family.
There can be a redemption only of that which has been for-
feited." [14] Religiously speaking, the clue to the creation of
man is his divine destiny. As Marsh sees it, only a created
man can be saved, and only in the whole context of creation
does the Christian gospel make sense.

" For an *evolved* man there is no hope of escaping the
chains of his bestial ancestors. His future attainments will,
by the nature of his past, of necessity be limited. But before every *fallen* man who repents and accepts the prof-
fered redemption shines the most radiant hope of complete
reinstatement in the household of God. The facts of Genesis not only find complete harmony with the facts of nature, they also penetrate and explain the mysteries of the
future." [15]

Hooper and Marsh accuse the evolutionists of having
merely a philosophical construct, but they themselves have
advanced philosophical arguments to refute it. Nowhere have
they dug into the scientific materials at hand, into the constantly growing body of experimental evidence bearing on
the problem. They illustrate pointedly how strong a driving
urge a religious conviction, be it right or wrong, can be — so
strong in fact that it will color an individual's use of factual
material at hand.

Even more regrettable, however, is the fact that these men
have felt called to defend a use of Biblical revelation long
since rejected by sound Biblical theology. No longer do theologians regard the meaning of Genesis as hanging or falling
on its accuracy as a scientific text. Revelation is not a substitute for what can be discovered scientifically, but rather a
perspective regarding the meaning of man's origin, and the

relationship of God to the life of his creatures. The validity of the theory of evolution is a scientific validity, and no insight regarding it can be gained by arguments from Biblical evidence. The validity of the Biblical record as a portrayal of God's relationship to man can be conceived independently of its scientific accuracy, and its meaning is not enhanced (but is rather perverted) by stretched attempts to give it a scientific validity it was not meant to have.

In what could be regarded as a footnote to this chapter, since the classification "creationist" hardly fits, belongs an interesting mid-position on the relation of evolution to religion. Louis Trenchard More, onetime professor of physics in the University of Cincinnati, in the Vanuxem Lectures at Princeton, January, 1925, accepts evolution as a biological theory but rejects it as the basis for a metaphysical interpretation of reality. These lectures, published under the title, *The Dogma of Evolution*,[16] occupy a mid-position between thinkers discussed in Chapter IV and those discussed in this chapter.

More points out that no consistently uniform interpretation has followed from the acceptance of evolution:

" Darwin's theory of evolution by natural selection, after the first attacks made on it by a shocked clergy, was passionately preached by men of the most different points of view. The captains of industry attached its flag to their masts because they found natural selection gave them the right to exploit the less endowed of their fellow men; the humanitarians and social workers used it as a shibboleth for the equality and brotherhood of men; the irreligious pointed to it as a proof that no god ruled the world; the clergy preached it from the pulpit as not inconsistent with the teachings and life of Jesus; the pacifists claimed it; and the warriors of the Nietzschean school of the superman justified the attempt of the Germans for world domination by its doctrine." [17]

More has no quarrel with the biological law that suggests that "species are mutually related in such a way that those forms now in existence are modified forms of previous species." [18] This he regards as a general law of biological science, demonstrable by the facts. He does quarrel, however, with the theory of natural selection, since this is really a metaphysical and unverifiable hypothesis. He strongly opposes the monism growing out of the theory of evolution which suggests all life processes are to be understood in mechanistic terms. He does not approve of the use of evolution as a key to the understanding of the social and ethical life of man; he feels that this only creates confusion.

More identifies himself with the Christian faith, but he does so in an entirely different way from the creationists. There is no trace of Biblicism in More; he even gives the evolutionist "the great credit of having, by ridicule, convinced us that the Christian religion had encrusted itself with a mass of superstitious beliefs in God and the Bible which could not withstand the facts brought to light by science." [19] But More makes a place for Christian faith. "Nor do I think," he writes, "that the materialism of the ordinary convert to evolutionary science is any more critical or any sounder in its blind acceptance of scientific hypotheses than is the idealism of the ignorant and credulous Christian." [20] That More keeps a certain dialectical freedom in viewing the relationship of science to Christianity is evidenced as he makes this suggestion: "The history of science is the same wayward chronicle of human effort and human mistakes as is that of philosophy and religion." [21]

More's understanding of man and culture bears more affinity to that of orthodox Christianity than to that of much evolutionary philosophy. In this regard he takes issue with the evolutionary philosophies of Spencer, Darwin, Huxley, Haeckel, and Fiske. He strongly denounces the mechanistic theory of life and conduct that springs from a monism that is ruled by scientific hypothesis and is backed by evolutionary presuppositions. In comparing the sociologists to the physicists, he makes this stinging comment:

" Scientific sociologists point to the laws of physics as a proof that individual chance can be subordinated to general laws. And they argue that they, too, can follow the same method when their science will have arrived at maturity. The question actually is, has their science ever been born? They make this parallel out of their abysmal ignorance of physics. Suppose we accept the law of physics that the pressure of a gas is due to the impact of an indefinitely large number of swiftly moving particles against the wall of the containing vessel. The necessary assumptions, according to Clerk Maxwell, that this law may hold are: The number of individuals must be indefinitely large; they must be all like; they must be so far apart that the action of any one will not affect the actions of any others; if any individual were withdrawn from or added to the vessel, the pressure would not be changed. These assumptions are necessary parts of the mathematical law of probability and chance. They cannot now, and never can, be made about the individual members of society." [22]

More does not believe in the idea of social progress, or what we have called moral evolution. " From a biological conception the Greeks were not as fit as the Hottentots for they could not maintain themselves, largely on account of the complexity of their organization, and the Hottentots still persist: sociologically, there is no doubt which was the more perfect type." [23] More also criticizes the criteria of progress used to support the idea of social and moral evolution. He disagrees with the idea that a heterogeneous society is more progressive than a simple society — the simple society may have the higher ideals. He also criticizes the whole concept that industrialization is morally significant. He has sharp words, perhaps surprising from a physicist, for purely technical education that eclipses the great liberal arts.

More believes that all future ethical achievement will be but a recapturing of the ethical and spiritual attainments of the prophets, seers, and saints of the past. He places Christ at the top of those who have attained. More is not clear as to whether he conceives of this religious situation in purely ethical terms. He gives a great place to the supernatural ("extra-mechanical") world, and the power of this world in the life of the saints. But, in speaking of the work of Christ, he does not formulate a religious doctrine of atonement. His view is more of an ethical idealism that sees conformance to a divine will and law already achieved in Christ than it is a theory of guilt and redemption. It is of major interest to us in this chapter because it is a religious outlook taking issue with evolution, not so much as biological fact, but as an interpretative principle.

So much for the footnote. The main discussion of the chapter has studied a creationism that seeks to reconcile the literal meaning of Biblical statements with scientific facts. There is another group of scientists, in the main more competent than the creationists, who likewise seek to find agreement between the Bible and science. They are united in an organization known as the American Scientific Affiliation, the work of which is sufficiently widespread to make necessary a separate chapter for its consideration. It is type B of the attempted reconciliation of Biblical statement and scientific fact.

VIII

BIBLICAL STATEMENT AND SCIENTIFIC FACT:

The American Scientific Affiliation

" *The Objects of the American Scientific Affiliation are:*
(1) *To integrate and organize the efforts of many individuals desiring to correlate the facts of science and the Holy Scriptures.*
(2) *To promote and encourage the study of the relationship between the facts of science and the Holy Scriptures.*
(3) *To promote the dissemination of the results of such studies.*"
— The Constitution of the ASA.[1]

THE American Scientific Affiliation is a fraternal organization of scientists holding a conservative view of Scriptural authority and seeking to exploit every opportunity to accord the facts of modern science with the literal content of the Biblical record. Not only in the matter of evolution, as the creationists, but at every point of possible overlap between science and Scripture, the concern of the ASA members makes itself felt.

Membership in the organization, which includes highly competent and sophisticated scientists, is of two grades: the associate, for which the prerequisite is an academic degree in a scientific field, and the fellow, the normal prerequisite for which is a doctorate. Equivalent experience may be accepted in lieu of the academic requirements. Certain doctrinal standards are imposed upon members. Associates sign the following brief statement:

"I believe the whole Bible as originally given to be the

inspired work of God, the only unerring guide of faith and conduct. Since God is the Author of this Book, as well as the Creator and Sustainer of the physical world about us, I cannot conceive of discrepancies between statements in the Bible and the real facts of science. Accordingly, trusting in the Lord Jesus Christ, the Son of God, my Saviour, for strength, I pledge myself as a member of this organization to the furtherance of its task." [2]

Fellows, who may be elected after one year as associates, accept a stronger statement of Biblical inspiration. They affirm faith in the Trinity, the divinity and Virgin birth of Christ, regeneration by the Holy Spirit, salvation by faith as against works, the inevitable choice between eternal blessedness and eternal punishment, and the Second Coming of Christ.

The membership of the ASA includes mostly scientists, though a few men working in other fields are on the rolls. We cannot list many names here, but to note the membership of the 1950 Executive Council will give an adequate flavoring. It included Dr. F. Alton Everest, associate director of the Moody Institute of Science; Dr. Allan A. MacRae, president of Faith Theological Seminary; Dr. Russell L. Mixter, chairman of the Department of Biology and professor of zoology in Wheaton College, Illinois; Dr. Roger J. Voskuyl, dean of Wheaton College and himself a chemist; and Dr. J. Laurence Kulp, assistant professor of geology in Columbia University.

The activity of the Affiliation includes holding a yearly conference for the reading of papers and the exchange of views. Five of these conferences have been held. Typical papers from the 1949 conference, held at the Biblical Institute of Los Angeles, included: a paper by Delbert N. Eggenberger, research chemist for Armour and Company, suggesting how Gamow's theory of neutron capture bolsters a belief in creation *ex nihilo;* a paper by Dr. Kulp describing the Carbon 14 method of dating; a paper by Dr. A. Van der Ziel, associate professor of physics, University of British Columbia, strongly advocating a realistic view of the descriptive function of science as contrasted with a view of science as philosophical inquiry into the " nature " of things; and a paper by a medical doctor in West Virginia, pointing out similarities between root meanings of Hebrew and Greek words in the Bible and words associated with modern atomic research.

The abstracts of these papers reveal two levels of concern. A few of the men are ready to deal scientifically with a subject regardless of its consequences for religious dogma. Thus Dr. Kulp, in his paper on the Carbon 14 method, indicates that Neanderthal remains can be dated as far back as 25,000 years. Here Kulp is willing to follow scientific fact even though it contradicts a traditional creationism, which, on Scriptural grounds, dates human origins around 4004 B.C.

The other extreme in the group is represented in the paper dealing with similarities between Hebrew and Greek words and certain terms used in atomic science. What possible meaning can be derived from the stretched observation that the Greek word for heaven and the English uranium have a similar root?

In addition to papers and conferences, the ASA has published a book, *Modern Science and Christian Faith*,[3] in which a fuller treatment of its view of the relationship of science and religion is given. Following the introduction by Dean Voskuyl, which holds that " A Christian Interpretation of Science " requires (1) belief in creation, (2) acceptance of the twofold character of revelation (through nature and through the Scripture), and (3) an understanding of human sin, the volume goes on to consider each science in turn: astronomy, geology, biology, anthropology, archaeology, medical science, chemistry, psychology, and physics. All the authors [4] are members of the ASA and are motivated by its basic urge to reconcile Biblical statement and scientific fact.

"It is the earnest prayer of each author that this volume will prove to be an able witness to the veracity of the Word of God in order that the claims of Christ on the lives of men may be effectively proclaimed in this science-minded age." [5]

The contributions in this symposium are of varying degrees of significance. The chapter on "The Bible and Chemical Knowledge" discusses the comparatively few references to chemical processes contained in Scripture and points out that these are basically in agreement with modern scientific knowledge. While the author of this chapter remains true to his chemical principles, his investigation seems superficial, if not meaningless. He notes, for example, that wherever the word "nitre" appears in the Bible, the description of its action correctly fits that of soda, and that "nitre" no doubt refers to the natron, a mixture of impure sodium carbonate and sodium bicarbonate, collected around the alkaline lakes of Egypt. The chapter is a series of like illustrations and ends:

"In conclusion we may say that the references to chemistry in the Bible are few, but are scientifically and historically accurate as we would expect in a book inspired of God. . . . The absence of chemical errors in the Bible only confirms our faith in the Holy Record." [6]

A more fruitful discussion, however, is in the chapter "A Christian View of Anthropology." Here great stress is laid upon the concept of the "supercultural" rather than the "supernatural." The writers of this chapter speak as follows:

"The term 'supercultural' . . . highlights the basic problem: what parts of our faith are man-made, developing through the natural processes of cultural dynamics, and what are divinely revealed and ordained? The great difficulty in studying the question lies in the fact that the revelation came in cultural form, and changed its clothes as culture changed through the years over which revelation occurred. Just as it is difficult to separate man as a biological organism from man as a creature of culture, so it is difficult to separate the Christianity of historical 'accident' from the Christianity of the supercultural." [7]

The awareness here of a distinction between the cultural and the supercultural deals with the same issue that much contemporary theology phrases as the distinction between God's word and man's. The fundamentalist motivation strong in the ASA estranges it, by either open denial or subconscious default, from these other theological movements, which, though they accept higher criticism, acknowledge the distinction between culture and revelation. Can it be that the authors of this volume, whose statement above is ample evidence of their thoughtfulness on this problem, tacitly reject the implied premise of the ASA — that the scientific material in the Bible must somehow belong in the supercultural? Would it not be more in harmony with their principles to note that the scientific materials in Scripture, as the wording of Scripture, are themselves culturally colored, and, therefore, incidental to the meaning of revelation? Is there not a failure here to follow through the implications of their own position and accept higher criticism?

However this may be, the writers of this chapter have much to say of real helpfulness. Not only do they carefully suggest that the science of anthropology can be separated from its current identity with naturalistic presuppositions and its a priori non-Christian judgments, but they have significant warnings to offer to those in the Christian fold. What theological thinker would not be grateful for the following contribution:

"A careful Christian thinker will realize that both 'projection of culture' and 'domestication of the universe' occur in Christian thinking to a greater or less degree depending upon the sophistication of the thinker. We are all too prone to interpret God in our own image rather than realizing that the picture which he has given of himself who is on the supercultural level has to be expressed in cultural terms in order to be intelligible to us who live on a cultural level." [8]

The fact that two temperaments are found in the ASA is a foreshadow of deeper rifts to come in the broader picture of the religion of scientists. The underlying religious philosophy of the creationists and the men in the ASA is a faith in the reconcilability of Biblical statement and scientific fact. But suppose one becomes convinced that a literal reading of the Bible cannot possibly be harmonized with the content of modern science, and suppose, further, that one is unwilling because of this to forswear religious faith? Two options would appear to be open. The first, to talk theology in theological language and science in scientific language, and to avoid joining the two. No scientist would take this course explicitly and avowedly; yet men can be found who are competent in the scientific field and who espouse a religious Biblicism in terms that never come to grips with the issues between science and religion. Their religious credos are simple statements of faith containing no reference to the reconciliations sought in all outlooks discussed thus far. The other alternative, to be discussed in chapter XI, is to find a dialectical reconciliation between the essential value judgments and religious outlook of Biblical faith and the world picture of modern science. This is the path followed in much contemporary neosupernaturalist theology and we find it appearing (as early as 1922) in writings of responsible natural scientists.

IX

COMPARTMENTALISM

" I put my Bible to the practical test of noting what it says about itself, and then tested it to see how it worked. . . .
" The outcome of such an experiment has been in due time the acceptance of the Bible as the Word of God inspired in a sense utterly different from any merely human book, and with it the acceptance of our Lord Jesus Christ as the only begotten Son of God, Son of Man by the Virgin Mary, and the Saviour of the world." [1] — Howard Atwood Kelly.

A TENSION between science and faith can be avoided by constructing two watertight compartments in one's thinking, one for religious matters, the other for scientific knowledge. The same individual may talk of science and of religion — even in the same breath — and not face the issues of their relationships to each other or of the historical conflicts that have occurred between them. When this happens, religion and science are compartmentalized and allowed to go their separate ways.

Dr. Howard Atwood Kelly, former professor of gynecological surgery at Johns Hopkins University, thus splits science and religion into two worlds. His position in religious matters has been made known in two pamphlets, one published by the American Tract Society and the other by the Great Commission Prayer League. The fuller statement of his thought is found in his book *A Scientific Man and the Bible,* published by the Sunday School Times Company.[2]

Kelly is a recognized scientist of no mean repute, and if one thumbs through the entries under his name in the card catalogue of a general library, he will find many entries for scientific works on medicine. But if one thumbs through his pamphlets or his book no scientific material appears, except incidental references to the fact that he is a doctor, and has " followed the developments of archaeology, geology, astronomy, herpetology, and mycology with a heavy appreciation of the advances being made in these fields." [3] There is no attempt to relate scientific medical knowledge to the religious subject matter at hand; the writings are merely " a personal testimony."

In A Scientific Man and the Bible, Kelly relates how he came to his present faith. Influential were the piety of his mother and the Philadelphia revival meetings at which Moody preached and Sankey sang. It was confirmed by talking about Christ to nonbelieving cowboys while on a rest cure in Colorado. During an illness with snow blindness Kelly underwent a profound experience. He relates it thus:

" There came as I sat propped up in my bed an overwhelming sense of a great light in the room and of the certainty of the near presence of God, lasting perhaps a few minutes and fading away, leaving a realization and a conviction never afterwards to be questioned in all the vicissitudes of life whatever they might be, a certainty above and beyond the processes of human reasoning." [4]

During, and right after, Kelly's internship higher criticism developed. In Kelly's eyes it made impossible faith in miracles, the Virgin birth, deity, atoning death, resurrection, and present mediatorial office of Christ. Higher criticism left Kelly " shivering in the cold," and he was forced back to a fervent faith in the Bible. The particular point at which Kelly's faith in the Biblical record took firm root in opposition to higher criticism was over the authorship of the Gospel of

John. Suggesting that the higher critics surely overreached themselves in dating John's Gospel about 150, Kelly remarks:

"Now, if any part of the Bible is assuredly the very Word of God speaking through his servant, it is John's Gospel. To ask me to believe that so inexpressibly marvelous a book was written long after all the events by some admiring follower, and was not inspired directly by the Spirit of God, is asking me to accept a miracle far greater than any of those recorded in the Bible." [5]

Kelly devotes an entire chapter to his belief that the whole Bible is the Word of God. " I am happy to say," he writes, " I do not have to pare and trim and make exceptions and allowances; constant use has taught me to accept the whole Bible as God's Word just as I took the letter received today as coming direct and without interpolations from my mother in Philadelphia." [6]

Kelly suggests that only by taking as a working hypothesis the Bible's own dictum about itself as God's infallible word is the richness of the Biblical message to be understood. This testing of the Word on its own terms is for Kelly the high fulfillment of " pragmatism." The essence of pragmatism is testing truth in terms of practical consequences. The practical consequences of Bible-reading are transforming. Such reading, " when applied with an honest heart, transforms the nature, ennobles the prostitute to love holiness and become an angel of mercy, [and] raises the beggar and the sot from the gutter to set them among the princes of the earth." [7]

The final guide of interpretation is God. When one first begins to read the Bible, his enthusiasm for the task and his zealousness in prayer make him strong in the Word. Older Christians become stale and weak, because they do not willingly put the responsibility upon God. It is this role of God as final interpreter of all truth that makes the Biblical message real and vital.

The self-authenticating character of Scripture, which fulfills both the test of pragmatism and constantly reveals God's own message, comes from the miraculous character of the Biblical record — "born in parts in the course of the ages yet completed in one harmonious whole." [8] It comes, too, from the fact that the Bible "is food for the spirit just as definitely as bread and meat are food for the body." [9] Or again, the Bible vindicates itself "because it is such excellent medicine; it has never yet failed to cure a single patient if only he took his prescription honestly." [10] The disease that the Bible cures is the "pandemic leprosy of the soul called sin." [11] In all this "the Bible alone brings the hungry soul into sweet concourse with the mind of God and so gives strength to bear trials and even to rejoice in misfortunes." [12]

Kelly extends his statement of faith to include belief in the deity of Christ, the Virgin birth, the blood atonement, the resurrection of the body, and the Second Coming. That Kelly makes of these the cardinal points of faith, together with his strong faith in Biblical literalism, clearly places him in the category of Protestant fundamentalism.

Each of these cardinal points is treated in a separate chapter. The general outline of the argument is similar in each case. The Biblical record and its authority are crucial, and on the basis of these Kelly takes his stand. Scientific challenges or problems raised by modern knowledge are occasionally mentioned, but summarily dismissed. In examining contemporary theories of evolution, for example, Kelly makes this treatment:

"Lost thus in sin and indifferent to his ancestry, man traces it along the gamut of the animal creation through multiplied millions of years, until he arrives in an Archean ooze of the Palaeozoic seas, where arriving at an impasse, namely, how life got into the ooze, he leaps lightly over the infinite gulf which separates life from death and postulates that primordial organic eozoon as a natural product of the hitherto eternally dead matter, or he even looks up into the infinite space of the starry heavens for some microscopic life germs conveyed to earth on a meteoric chariot of fire." [13]

While the evidence that Kelly works from isolated religious authority piles up in each of the chapters, nowhere is the compartmentalization of his religious philosophy so clearly shown as in the treatment of the Virgin birth. Kelly, it will be recalled, is a highly competent professor of gynecology at Johns Hopkins. The fourth chapter of his book is a series of theological arguments for the Virgin birth based on Biblicistic presuppositions. There is no discussion at all about the scientific possibility of a Virgin birth, no attempted reconciliation between scientific fact and Biblical statement. There is merely a statement of belief in the Virgin birth based upon the Biblical record and Early Church practice, concluding with these words:

" The Virgin birth is a fact fully established by competent testimony and abundant collateral evidences, believed by men all through the ages as a necessary factor in their salvation secured by an everliving, ever-acting Saviour, viewed with wonder by angels in heaven and acknowledged by the Father. To deny the Virgin birth because of its miraculous nature is to deny the validity of all Scripture, which is but a continuous series of revelations of the mind and acts of God, and as such is miraculous throughout." [14]

Kelly betrays a continual concern that the basis of religious faith be unshakable. He suggests again and again that to let down bars at one place is to invite the destruction of the whole edifice. Thus, the Bible must be taken as a whole, or not at all; Christ must be accepted as fully divine, and actually born of a virgin, or not at all; eschatology must be seen as the prediction of the earthly and historical return of Christ, or have no meaning at all. No challenge from scientific theory must be allowed to shake this body of truth. It stands alone, and there is, therefore, no urgent necessity for understanding the relationships between scientific and religious epistemology. They are — though Kelly does not use this term, nor explicitly regard this as the accurate description of his thought — compartmentalized.

Protestant orthodoxy, since it finds in the Bible a full and complete system of religious truth, lends itself easily to compartmentalization. Extreme fundamentalism will state its case, as we have seen in Kelly, in unequivocal terms. Compartmentalization need not, however, take such an extreme form. It is possible to discuss both scientific and religious issues in the same work, and yet leave each to its own sphere. Charles M. A. Stine, Director of Research for E. I. Du Pont de Nemours & Co. from 1907 to 1945 does this. His book *A Chemist and His Bible* [15] deals with both Biblical writings and modern science.

Stine works somewhat as follows: He takes a Biblical text and describes its obvious meaning. Then he takes a corresponding scientific fact and shows how it points to the same truth by an entirely different method. For example, the first chapter of Genesis is a statement of the wonderful character of God's creation. But science too points to the wonder of the universe. Hence, the wonder of the universe is common to both, and the Bible speaks of it in one way, science in another.

Or again, the Bible speaks of man in these terms: " I will praise thee; for I am fearfully and wonderfully made: marvelous are thy works; and that my soul knoweth right well." [16] Modern science supports this judgment from an entirely different ground of understanding. Our chemical knowledge of the body shows that it is a most complex chemical factory, and thus wonderfully made. Again, Scripture and science agree. Or, to take another instance, in Isaiah 40:12 we read: "Who hath measured the waters in the hollow of his hand, and meted out heaven with the span, and comprehended the dust of the earth in a measure, and weighed the mountains in scales, and the hills in a balance?" (K.J.V.), and from this we know that great hidden treasure is to be found in God's provision of water on the earth. But we know from science that without water there could be no life. Hell (in which we must believe as a corollary of heaven since we cannot believe in just one part of God's inspired book) would surely be a place without water.

Or yet again, in Hebrews we read, " Through faith we understand that the worlds were framed by the word of God, so that things which are seen were not made of things which do appear." [17] And from our science, independently, we know that " the chemists say matter is composed of something that we describe as electric charges, or electricity . . . the building blocks of atoms." [18] Do we not therefore find a common element in the two paths?

But is this not a unity of science and faith rather than a compartmentalism? In a way; though it takes no cognizance of the historical tensions between Biblical statement and scientific fact. Stine does not seek to reconcile a literal interpretation of Scripture with scientific knowledge even though he holds to both. Nevertheless, in another book [19] Stine, together with Milton H. Stine, a minister, tries to deal with this problem. Here he swings into the creationist camp. Consideration of the scientific issues involved is so far overshadowed by the affirmation of the Biblical record as inspired fact that one can hardly look at the book without suspecting a dualism.

In this book the first chapter is devoted to the scientific evidence. It is hardly a critical or full inquiry, and it bases its final critique of evolution on religious grounds — that evolved man did not fall, hence needs no redeemer; that an evolved man cannot be the object of that love of God depicted in the whole Bible; and that finally evolution and materialistic socialism are in the same camp.

" It is a remarkable fact that the basic idea underlying this false philosophy [of evolution] is also the regnant idea underlying socialism, which teaches that man is organically and essentially one with God and the universe. It is easy to foresee tremendous results from what, at first sight, seem two systems entirely opposite in thought and aim." [20]

The five succeeding chapters are religious affirmations without any reference to the relationship of science and faith. Stine gives the impression that, once one has broken free from the doctrine of evolution, no barriers exist for a conservative Christian faith. Accordingly, chapter II stresses the infallibility of the Biblical word, the religious meaning of the historical fall of Adam, and the divinity of Christ and his work. Chapter III discusses the problem of suffering and suggests that God will overcome the enigma. The fourth chapter discusses prayer; the fifth, the cultivation of piety; and the sixth, the life to come.

Religious authority is Biblical. It is based upon a reading of the Bible as God's own word. The Bible is self-sufficient and complete; religious truth is self-vindicating. " We believe," write the Stines, " in the plenary inspiration of the Scriptures, inspired in their entirety and every part. It is obviously therefore a book which contains utterances which are historically and scientifically correct." [21] Surely this is a clear statement of autonomous religious faith.

Stine does not belong with those whose concern for the reconciliation of science and faith drives them to ever new investigation. He belongs rather to the group that again and again affirms the infallible status of the Biblical writings. Speaking of his study of chemistry and other sciences in relation to his reading of the Bible, he suggests that both have "engendered in my mind a constantly increasing appreciation of the wisdom stored in the God-inspired pages of the old Book." [22] This is no more true than in the following quotation, written immediately after observing that because we cannot scientifically understand the full nature of light, we ought to appreciate the possibility that Moses' face shone miraculously as recorded in the thirty-fourth chapter of Exodus:

> "It is the writer's desire only to take the glorious and wonderful words of the Bible to deepen our reverence for His majesty and glory and wisdom and power and transcendent perfection. Prayerful and reverent meditation upon the Scriptures describing appearances of God to his servants should serve to deepen our love and increase our humility." [23]

Compartmentalization comes from an attempt to gloss over the problems between science and faith. It comes when the issue is made acute by a religious view of Biblical statements that supposes them to carry scientific authority. It becomes dominant when obvious discrepancies between the Biblical phrasing of cosmological concepts conflict with modern scientific theory. It is one means of handling a perplexing problem, but its cost is high in terms of the unabridged gulf between the two sides.

Fortunately, however, there is another way of dealing with the problem. It consists of a modification of one's view toward the Scripture. The modification does not reject Scriptural authority, but sees this authority in the spiritual rather than the verbal realm. It sees the Bible as the interpreter of existence, and as a word to human life applicable to every situation, but independent of the scientific facts involved. It can therefore openly face and dialectically resolve the conflict between Biblical statement and scientific fact. It can take a new concept of Biblical authority — that it speaks to the specifically religious situation of man, as much in our day as in the day when its now out-of-date scientific references were written — and can relate this to the world picture of modern science. It can, in short, find a reconciliation between Biblical faith (not Biblical record) and scientific fact.

X

SCIENTIFIC KNOWLEDGE AND BIBLICAL FAITH

" Three alternatives present themselves. You may hold by the authority of the Bible in the field of astronomy, geology, physics, chemistry, physiology, and biology, and flout the science of the time. Or you may reject the authority of the Bible in all fields on account of its discredit in the field of science. Or you may revise your conception of the origin and purpose of the Bible and so retain your reverence before its divine authority without embarrassment before the assured results of science. The last alternative is the only one which it is possible to adopt." [1]
— William Louis Poteat.

WE COME now to a group of scientists who are fully aware of discrepancies between the literal Biblical record and the findings of modern science. However, they are neither ready to overthrow the Bible as a central guide to religious faith nor to change their science to fit the Bible. They seek to reconcile contemporary scientific knowledge with a religious outlook based on the Biblical message. They accept the Bible as uniquely significant for Christian faith without taking it as verbally inspired and literally true.

These men do not all use identical arguments. One regards the Biblical stories as mythological; another regards them as true science for their own time, but not for ours. One slips into mild allegory; another keeps a stern and consistent dialectical method of interpretation; but they all finally come to a basic reconciliation between scientific knowledge and Biblical faith, a reconciliation in which each is accepted within its respective area of concern without being allowed to contradict the other.

Frederick J. Pack, former professor of geology at the University of Utah and author of *Science and Belief in God*, [2] is on the border line of such a dialectical position. He suggests that the completely skeptical, historical, humanistic viewpoint toward the Bible is no more valid than literalism. He suggests that we read the Bible with the attitude that God taught the ancient Israelites at their level of understanding. Thus, Biblical concepts about the natural world, while not in agreement with contemporary science and no longer true from a scientific standpoint today, nevertheless represent a picture of the natural world in harmony with " scientific " knowledge at the time of writing. Pack hesitates to use the term " myth " to describe the Biblical accounts, for myth, as he sees it, refers to stories known to be imaginative at the time of origin; Biblical stories are not deliberately imaginative, but simply " time-bound."

At places Pack sounds almost like a literalist, suggesting that we have certain geologic evidence pointing to a flood that covered the Holy Land area known to the writer of Genesis; but, unlike the literalist, Pack does not regard the scientific matter involved as crucial for Biblical authority. He writes:

" The writer's views do not conform with the widespread belief that there is no real historical background for the Biblical story of the deluge, nor does he believe that a strictly literal interpretation is necessary to its acceptance." [3]

Pack makes much of the fact that the Biblical record permits great freedom of interpretation. Evidently reading the " P " rather than the " J " version of Genesis, he comments about creation as follows:

" It should be apparent to careful readers that the Biblical narrative does not attempt to explain the manner of man's origin. On the other hand, it emphasizes the fact that God is the author of man's existence, and furthermore, that man was fashioned in the form of Deity. Elsewhere the record even states that human beings are his " offspring." [4]

A suggestion of this type deliberately side-steps the technical matter involving creation as a method and emphasizes instead a theological judgment about God's place in creation and man's situation as a child of God. Pack goes farther. Evolution may properly describe the development of life, but the scientist has not yet learned how to investigate the question of the origin of life. The ultimate explanation of life is based upon the revelation that God is its true author, but this dictates no dogma regarding the mode of its development.

In this reconciliation of Biblical faith and the doctrine of evolution, Pack comes close to the men we looked at in chapter IV. He is distinguished from them, not so much by his attitude toward evolution as by his own admission that his ideas are Biblically rooted rather than based upon a general philosophical inquiry into scientific evidence. How closely Pack comes in the content of his thought to the men finding in evolution a central religious meaning is shown in Pack's occasional statement to the effect that man is forever bettering himself. Yet this too has a religious flavor:

" Even religion, the choicest thing in the world, consists of a systematic series of efforts designed to place its adherents outside the field of wrongdoing and within the field of right. By continuous activity along certain lines it is believed that individuals will eventually become immune to the influences of evil, and that finally they will respond only to that which is noble and true. Then, even

in matters of religion, unchangeability does not exist, other-
wise eternal betterment would be impossible." [5]

That Pack slips back, at places, into stretched methods
of reconciliation, will come as a disappointment to those who
find his treatment of evolution satisfying. At one place he
goes so far as to suggest that because water contains hydrogen and oxygen, whereas wine contains hydrogen, oxygen,
and carbon, the transformation of one to the other at the
feast of Cana, in a world with carbon easily available, is not
too strange a miracle to have taken place. Less stretched,
perhaps, are his interpretations in which he supports his idea
of eternal consciousness by pointing to the indestructibility
of matter or the literal resurrection of the body on the
grounds that it does not demand the reappearance of the
identical flesh and bone of its original at the time of death.

Pack's ethics tend to be puritanistic. They are not spelled
out in any full sense, but the general temper of them can be
inferred from the following quotation, which Pack gives as
the reasons for loss of religious faith on the campus:

"It cannot be denied that certain student 'functions'
are deleterious to religious devotion. Week-end dances,
with their not infrequent tendency to run over into Sunday morning, make a very poor preparation for the proper
observance of the Sabbath Day. 'Busts,' at which tobacco
and even liquor are sometimes urged upon those present,
are far from uplifting in their general influence. The use
of profanity seems to be considered a manly act among certain classes of college men." [6]

Pack's general approach is also found in the thought of
Dr. Charles E. de M. Sajous, professor of endocrinology in
the University of Pennsylvania Graduate School of Medicine.
Sajous wrote at the same time as Pack, and starts his work
with a consideration of the same moral decadence Pack re-

fers to in the quotation above. Sajous points to the rising crime wave in the America of the mid-twenties and suggests that it can be stopped only by religion. He then analyzes the main causes of atheism and finds that an intellectual stumbling block to faith — the literal interpretation of the Bible — is causing many intellectually honest people to reject Christianity. He asks, in light of this:

" Why not rid the Bible, as far as present knowledge will permit, of modes of interpretation justly calculated to fit the relatively childish and illiterate minds of primitive times, but which today only serve to obscure the true sense of the text and conceal its spiritual origin? Once rid of these repellent versions, *the Biblical text will glow as a great white light* and irresistibly draw to it not only previously professed atheists, but also the millions of individuals of both sexes and of all classes who today are quite indifferent to religious teachings." [7]

Sajous proceeds to work out an interpretation of Scripture that will fit the demands of modern science. He believes that errors in the translation of the original Hebrew text are largely responsible for the irreconcilability of the Biblical accounts of creation with the findings of modern science. Therefore he proposes a series of retranslations that will reconcile the Scripture with scientific insight. Taking his suggestions for Genesis 2:7 as representative, let us look at his method. The King James Version reads, " And the Lord God formed man of the dust of the ground, and breathed into his nostrils the breath of life; and man became a living soul." Sajous' translation becomes, " Andformed God theman dust fromtheground andbreathed innostrilshis breathspirit and became theman a soulspirit." [8]

This second translation, by using the terms " breathspirit " and " soulspirit," rather than " man " and " living soul," shows that a symbolic sense is meant rather than a report of a historical event. Thus, man's life is symbolically derived from God's soulspirit, and the Bible in its original meaning — and as it impressed its contemporaries — was written in a purely symbolical sense. It did not mean to recount a historical event; it does not contain a myth, that is an imaginative story, but a purely symbolic value judgment. This distinction between myth and symbolic value judgment seems overdrawn; are not the two, at least as we must read them, one and the same? As the idea of myth is used in current theological thought does it not convey precisely this idea of symbolic value judgment?

Sajous applies this same general technique to the story of the Fall and shows that "Adam" and "Eve" are not meant as specific individuals, but as mankind in general. The story of the Fall becomes "*a solemn plea to mankind to beware of the animal instincts* which the animal inheritance of the body includes." [9] Here again Sajous so interprets the Bible as to leave a place for the scientific account of man's origin. By confining the story of the Fall to the simple religious category of a warning against sin, he avoids having to deal with the historicity of the event, thus running into conflict with science.

Pack, while willing to free himself of a dogma of verbalism, is too ready to consider the possibility of reconciling early Biblical science with current data. Sajous' method of retranslation seems not only to stretch the Hebrew but also to offer little promise of adequacy to cover all the possible reconciliations of modern science and Biblical cosmologies. In a contemporary of these men, however, Henry Higgins Lane, professor of zoology at the University of Kansas, there is to be found a more sophisticated attempt to reconcile a scientific theory and Biblical faith. His book, *Evolution and Christian Faith*,[10] written in 1923, comes close to the mood of much contemporary Christian theology. It accepts the scientific theory of evolution on the scientific evidence involved and devotes the first 121 pages to a straight scientific discussion. It then seeks to probe the meaning of the Biblical message in regard to its doctrine of man and in Part II puts forth a carefully reasoned statement of Christian faith as derived from its Biblical roots. Thus Lane concludes:

" The very least that could be said of the relation of evolution to Christianity would be that they are incommensurables, and as such evolution leaves the Christian religion exactly where it has always been, *free to stand or fall upon the evidence for its divine origin.* The doctrine of evolution presents no difficulties too great to be harmonized with the gospel of Christ." [11]

Evolution does not, as Lane sees it, preclude religious faith, but rather reinforces such a faith. However, faith is not derived from evolution, but from its Biblical roots. " *Evolution is God's method of operation in the realm of nature; Christianity is God's plan of operation in the spiritual world.*" [12] Thus, while separately derived, they are finally caught up in a fuller truth embracing both scientific and religious aspects.

" The salvation of the world depends upon the discovery of the ground where the imperishable truths of both science and religion may be found to dovetail together into a complete and harmonious whole. . . . The idea of creation by divine will without natural process is just as contrary to the facts as revealed by science, as is the opposite materialistic view of creation by natural process without divine will." [13]

Lane is sharp with the materialist who asserts that species were derived from nonliving matter through a happy concentration of circumstances — that they " just grew "; he is equally sharp with the literalistic and orthodox clergyman who asserts that species "were made out of hand by the Creator." The theistic evolutionist, who asserts that "*species were created by a process of evolution*" achieves that happy balance of scientific fact and Biblical faith for which Lane argues. In this regard Lane suggests that the bar to a speedy reconciliation between science and religion "is not in the head, but in the heart — is not in the reason, but in pride of opinion, self-conceit, dogmatism." [14] The dogmatism is not on one side. It appeared first on the theological side only because theology was first in power. "In modern times it has gone over to the side of science, because here now is the place of power and fashion." [15] Lane explains the popular belief in the antagonism of science and religion as due to the fact "that some atheists who are also evolutionists have been so vociferous in proclaiming their views." [16] "It is time," suggests Lane, "that the many scientists who are not materialists should make known their philosophy and religious faith." [17]

That Lane makes materialism synonymous with atheism no doubt reflects the intellectual climate of his day. He shows in his writings a strong disposition to favor idealistic philosophy, and since idealism was strong then and closely allied with Christian thought, this bias is easily understood. As to whether Lane is using idealism in the specifically technical sense, or merely as a convenient counterpart to materialism, we cannot be certain. One is tempted to interpret Lane's materialism more in terms of what now is viewed as mechanistic determinism and his idealism as any view that makes room for creative spiritual forces, for a living, acting deity, and for purpose at work in natural order.

Thus science deals only with sensible data, with the ponderable and measurable. It seeks only proximate, not ultimate, causes. The subject of ultimate causation belongs to philosophy, not science, and through philosophy to religion. In religion we learn from the Biblical message and from the interpretation of life that it portrays. This Biblical interpretation is not at odds with, or dependent upon, a scientific outlook and knowledge about the universe, but extends beyond it.

Again illustrating the philosophical position of this chapter from a scientist writing in the mid-twenties, we turn to the contribution of William Louis Poteat, the former professor of biology at Wake Forest College. Poteat's contribution to the understanding between science and religion is better known than is that of the other men we have discussed here, and his thought is more adequately crystallized. That Poteat undergirds his religious thought with a careful idea of the relationship between science and religion is immediately apparent in his book *The New Peace*.[18] A later, and even more fruitful, exposition of his own religious thought is found in the book, *Can a Man be a Christian Today?* [19] This is the printed form of the McNair Lectures at the University of North Carolina.

Poteat plunges to the heart of the matter with these words: " A man may be a Christian and accept the divine authority of the Bible for the religious life, and at the same time reject the world view for which it is sometimes made responsible." [20] By " world view," in this context, Poteat means the cosmological outlook of the Biblical writers.

Poteat uses strong words against both " the rationalization of science " that will " set down as absurd what it is unable to explain or handle with its apparatus of the foot rule, the clock, and the balance " [21] and fundamentalism, which rationalizes religious experience and represents a " conservatism putting in jeopardy the cause it seeks to save." [22] He asks, " Who regards religion as an explanation of nature, who but the literalists? " [23] To the secularists who believe nothing in the Bible, as well as to the literalists who profess to believe everything, Poteat cries, "'A plague o' both your houses!'"

Poteat is not suggesting, by any means, that there are no implications for religion in science. Science has faith in the understandable regularity of nature; this has religious significance. Science gives a place for intellectual adventure; who would exclude that from faith? Science gives a place for intellectual wonder; is this not indeed at the heart of the vision of faith? Faith is not assent to external truths, not credulous belief, but "the deep-lying capacity to apprehend the external world and respond to its appeal." [24] Thus a true continuity exists between the scientific attitude and the attitude of religion. Poteat suggests that Christianity can be looked at in four ways: (1) as an inward experience where "deep calleth unto deep"; (2) as a rule of life — that is, a moral standard; (3) as a body of teaching, subject to contemporary philosophical currents; and (4) as a historic movement, originating with the life, teachings, and death of Christ. The first two categories are more or less fixed; the second two, progressive and modified in light of current situations and demands.

Between the first set and the second a dialectic arises. Poteat knows full well that no easy or simple solution is offered the Christian Church to the problem of separating the chaff from the wheat in religious matters. Poteat knows that "in its passage through these twenty centuries from East to West, through varying levels of culture and types of social organization, everywhere meeting a new opportunity with a fit instrument of service, molding the situation but taking on some of its complexion, Christianity, from being simple and inchoate as it was at first, has come to be complex and elaborately organized. It has accumulated much baggage, useful and in most cases necessary, but baggage nevertheless, and baggage is not traveler." [25]

Thus Poteat cites as dangers to the Church unnatural al-

liances, elaborate liturgy and ritual, and elaborate speculation about Christian experience. He knows that the Church
can fall into three morasses: Biblical literalism, untenable
world views dictated by theological speculation, and intellectual consent to creedal proposition rather than " response
in love and loyalty to the appeal of Christ." Yet Poteat knows
that " Christianity could not have reached us without its ac-
cessories. It cannot now escape them wholly." [26] He knows
that while " the agencies and institutions of Christianity are
not Christianity, but its tools, . . . Christianity must have
its tools." [27] Thus Poteat becomes dialectical in theology as
well as in his reconciliation of scientific statement and Biblical faith, fruitfully suggesting a creative way of regarding
the tension between Christian faith and the outside culture,
between the essential gospel and its historical expression.

Poteat likewise understands the dialectic of ethical de-
cision. In discussing the relationship of scientific activity to
ethical concern, he says,

" pure science and its practical applications merely create
the conditions under which instinct and passion compass
their ends. Science confers power, not purpose. It is a blessing, therefore, if the purpose which it serves is good; it is
a curse, if the purpose is bad. It is clear, for example, that
if Christian conscience does not end war, science will end
civilization." [28]

And yet, despite this potential threat, science is tremendously
serving mankind and preparing in the wilderness the way of
the Lord. Thus, technology is a boon to man, but also his
potential undoing — both aspects must be pointed out in any
full analysis.

The four men already discussed in this chapter find the
content of their faith in Biblical insights. Their basic attitude
toward the relationship of science to religion is one that ad-

mits two spheres of authority, which nevertheless must be interrelated to each other.

A Roman Catholic parallel to this method of reconciling the truth of science with the truth of Scripture is found in the report of the Biblical Commission designated by the Vatican to deal with the problem of relating Scripture to science. Hugh S. Taylor, dean of the Graduate School and professor of chemistry at Princeton, quotes this report with the suggestion that it

" could well be emphasized by all science teachers counseling students in such matters: ' On those matters which form the proper object of the physical and natural sciences, God taught nothing to men by the intermediary of the sacred writers since such instruction could not be of any use for their eternal salvation.' " [29]

Taylor's view is more typically Catholic than Protestant, for while he, like Lane and Poteat, recognizes the need for two spheres of authority, he tends to regard the nature of religious authority more in philosophical than in Biblical terms. Thus:

" Science seeks the truth concerning the natural order. But there is a science outside her scope, a higher physics, a metaphysics, the science of those things which *are*, dissociated from material things, which can not only be conceived without matter but which can also exist without matter, the truths which man comprehends as the attributes of God." [30]

To understand the distinction between these two realms, to guard properly the limits of the scientific method, is the mark of the wise scientist. As Taylor sees it, science is powerless in deciding ethical questions, and of itself only secures proximate rather than ultimate truth.[31]

Taylor uses the argument from design in only a qualified sense. He understands that religious questions need religious answers and is wary of drawing metaphysical deductions from physical principles. Nevertheless he points out that "even in the sciences of physics and of chemistry many empirical observations do possess implication of design and purpose." [32]

In this suggestion Taylor moves close to the Christian theism discussed in chapter II, even as many of the men in that chapter, by relying in the final analysis upon religious authority where arguments based on scientific evidences produced ambiguous results, moved close to the men in this chapter. Taylor accepts the need of authority, and yet finds provisional truth in the argument from design. Arthur Compton, it will be remembered, in seeking to utilize the argument from design, came finally to rely upon the judgment of traditional authority.

Taylor, no less than the other men in this chapter, insists that "the faith of the Christian and the advance of scientific knowledge must be reconciled. The discoveries of science must be harmonized with the teachings of the Bible," [33] and also, "the necessary condition for the reforming of our civilization involves the reintegration of science into a unity with philosophy and religion." [34]

And so, Pack and Sajous, and more particularly Lane and Poteat, find a means to do full justice to scientific truth at the same time that they give basic allegiance to the place of Biblical faith. Taylor pleads for a reconciliation between both the Biblical and the philosophical content of Christian thought. But a religious reading of the Bible may not necessarily issue in such a dialectic system. Use can be made of certain specific parts of the Bible to support individual interpretations. In this type of religious philosophy Biblical faith is lost as a unit — as a whole and basic interpretation of reality — and in its place a particular idea is given support by reference to Biblical material. So clearly is this shown in the works by Igor Sikorsky, who uses the Bible to support an anti-materialist spiritualism, that we devote a final chapter to an exposition of his thought.

XI

THE PROTEST AGAINST MATERIALISM

" Religious thought proclaims that man is not a superbeast,
but a living being of a higher grade of life; that his qualifica-
tions, governing the miraculous ascent, are the consequence
of the presence of the supremely mysterious higher spiritual
life which is living spiritually in his physically living body." [1]
— Igor Ivan Sikorsky.

IN CHAPTER VI we discussed a pseudoreligious enthusiasm for science and invention. We traced the thought patterns that give expression to such enthusiasm and noted that
they herald the practical and material benefits of science with
thanksgiving and gratitude. We saw them make strong appeal for the steady and unlimited development of technology
and prophesy with great earnestness the future benefits of
the scientific enterprise.

Our attention now turns to a religious frame of mind that,
if not to be set in sheer opposition to that discussed in chapter VI, is surely to be seen in contrast with it. This protest
against materialism, which one finds most fully in the writings of the famous plane designer, Igor Sikorsky, emphasizes
the pursuance of spiritual value as the chief end of man. Man
should not hunt mammon, according to this view, nor pursue
worldly goods as his chief desire. Rather, he should cultivate
the inner, mystical, and nonmaterial values that alone en-
dure and distinguish man from the beasts.

Sikorsky's clearest treatment of this theme comes in his

small book *The Invisible Encounter,*[2] which is subtitled "A Plea for Spiritual Rather than Material Power as the Great Need of Our Day." The "invisible encounter" is the confrontation of Jesus by the devil in the temptation narratives. Sikorsky's interpretation of these narratives describes them as a clash between materialism and spiritual religion.

Sikorsky suggests that the devil's arguments, as he confronted Jesus in the temptation narratives, must have run somewhat as follows: "If you do not turn the stone into bread, that is, provide material food with which to feed the poor, they will turn against you, and your case will be lost. If you do not lead a physical and violent revolt against the yoke of Rome — while nevertheless claiming to be the Messiah — the priests will turn against you. If you cling to ideals, demanding strict allegiance to the stringent requirements of the Kingdom of God, instead of allowing compromise with family and patriotic obligations, you will sow seeds of great agony as you break up established institutions."

Sikorsky believes that the great and crucial issue between the devil and Christ was whether Christ would take a material or a spiritual road to the establishment of his Kingdom on earth. The devil suggested to Christ that mankind deserves concrete help in changing conditions of life in the world, and that Christ should concern himself with the meeting of material need. Thus the devil pleaded with Christ, as Sikorsky imagines it, to care for the material needs of the masses:

"In order to help mankind, in order really to unload the unbearable burden of suffering and at the same time open wide the way for quick spreading and accepting of Your own teaching, You must and can change their surroundings and conditions of life [for the masses] before attempting to change their souls."[3]

Materialism is demonic. In terms of the world crisis, " Nazism and Communism . . . are only the first manifestations, the early gentle flowers of radical intellectual materialism at work." [4] In Marxism, as Sikorsky sees it, concern for material plenty and for economic alleviation of the condition of the poor clearly overrides the spiritual emphasis that ought to be put on the dignity of the individual, the freedom of man, and the basic regard for personal and corporate integrity. In Communism the worship of mammon spills over into a lust for political domination, and materialism ends in tyranny.

This is a currently popular critique of Communism, but it hardly gets to the root of the issue. Communist totalitarianism does not spring simply from its materialism, as contrasted with religious spirituality, but from a perverted kind of spirituality. The ideology of the class war, the utopian aim of a classless society, and the drive for world "liberation" implicit in Communism are sufficiently nonmaterial. They are ideological elements used to justify every level of ethical contradiction needed to achieve the desired ends. Surely if the evil in either Fascism or Communism is simply its worship of material ends, the non-Communist world is as much at fault as the Communist one.

Sikorsky understands this to a great extent. He knows, following Spengler, that the infection has spread to the whole of technical civilization. Comparing this civilization with Goethe's Doctor Faust, who made a pact with the devil to gain domination over men in order to furnish earthly happiness to millions, he comments:

" The complete power over men and nature to be utilized for brave, humanitarian objectives is accepted and welcomed, while the reciprocative pact with the evil by which this power [is] gained is considered a meaningless allegory or completely ignored." [5]

But Sikorsky's treatment raises questions. Granted that Christ did not make a pact with the devil to establish an earthly kingdom, he was not unconcerned about the material wants of the poor. He fed the crowd of five thousand and commanded Simon Peter to feed his sheep. And what are we to make of Sikorsky's rigid distinction between the material and spiritual content of the Kingdom of God? This could be a veiled suggestion that the contemporary Church should concern itself with purely "religious" matters and manifest no concern for social righteousness and for the alleviation of the conditions of the poor and socially oppressed.

But accepting the view at its face value, as a basic distinction between the spiritual and the material, one still wonders why Sikorsky espouses it. Sikorsky is a practical scientist, an engineer, a production man. He is an executive, the manager of United Aircraft Manufacturing Corporation. Surely he deals again and again with the material side of life. Does he feel that religion must contrast sharply with the character and concerns of his daily work? Does he emphasize the spirituality of religion, as opposed to the materialism of science and technology, in a subconscious reaction to his professional situation?

Sikorsky's emphasis upon the spiritual includes an ethical idealism in which he asserts the need for strict allegiance to moral standards. "In light of moral principles and certainly from the Christian standpoint," Sikorsky writes, "means are frequently more important than ends." [6] Materialism leads to corruptions of ethical ideals, and only by overcoming the lies, self-deception, and bad will that now rule our world will moral order be re-established. The first rule of Christian life is, "Never lie to anyone and particularly not to yourself." This is sharply opposed to the frantic self-deception of modern life, and only by this moral steadfastness of the Christian faith can we be saved; it was such moral steadfastness that underlay the rise and power of early Christianity.

"While the eternal mystical meaning of Christ's message and sacrifice, and of original sin, are not discussed in this study, yet, with respect to earth realities, it is right to state that religious idealism and particularly the Christian faith provided the most powerful lifesaving serum, which protected men and nations from the deadly effects of the sinister spiritual evil that is always present and ready to strike, as soon as moral vigilance relaxes." [7]

Ethical weakness in materialism is backed by its philosophical and metaphysical weakness, and the second explains the first. Materialism believes, as Sikorsky sees it, that man is an animal with a brain two pounds heavier than the brain of other comparably sized beasts, that man has elevated himself by greater aggressiveness, and that power alone can be trusted. This estimate of man and his nature, which sells man out to natural instinct and brutal coercion is not the Christian view. " The gospel message stresses the infinite value of each individual human life, placing supreme emphasis on the spiritual side of it." [8] This intimate relationship between God and man and the care of the divine Father for each person as an individual are implied in the emphasis of the Lord's Prayer upon " Our Father." " To harmonize with [many medieval and some contemporary] concepts, the addressing words should have been ' Our eternal dictator and stern judge,' but thank God, this is not the case." [9]

There is a strain of mysticism in Sikorsky's thought, both toward the positive and the negative parts of spiritual reality. He speaks of a " mystical evil power," which captures men who do not hold fast to that which is good and those who do not ally themselves with positive mystical power in the world. This positive power is always available and will be the victor in any showdown.

" I am convinced that in the final plan of God, the power of life and truth is infinitely greater than the sum of evil. I believe that the immensity, orderliness, and beauty of the visible heaven-universe are but a dim reflection of the magnificence and harmony of the all-conquering, eternal, living universe of higher order. Whatever evil may come to us in this life is trivial when measured against the greatness, power, and splendor of the material and spiritual universe." [10]

Thus to participate, mystically if you will, in this higher order of reality and to know by faith that God will finally reign supreme is a present source of strength for daily living. The prayer, " Thy Kingdom come. Thy will be done in earth, as it is in heaven," comes from a life in full harmony with God. This type of life already exists in the universe, and the prayer is only an expressed trust that it would " descend and engulf our earth, [and that] the best part of mankind would then be lifted to the higher order of existence." [11] This is an eternal hope, in which

" man feels lifted to eminent heights of hope and gratitude to his Creator and Teacher who in some mysterious way opened the door from our little earth, that will eventually be destroyed with its contents, into the immensity and splendor of the heaven-universe. This is the deeply important and significant meaning of the first part of the Lord's Prayer." [12]

This spiritual resource gives us great steadfastness of spirit in a troubled time, since " no one can take this sublime meaning of life away from us, and this is the one thing that matters." [13]

In Sikorsky's thought science acquires significance as a study of God's handiwork and involves reverence and love for the Creator of the world. This does not preclude its function as a study of the earth in its own majesty and beauty, but it does suggest that only by passing beyond this natural world into a supernatural one — a spiritual world known with reverence and awe — does science become religiously significant. The Wise Men of old who came to Bethlehem — scientists by the standards of their own times — perceived this spiritual quality about the event of Christ's birth. Because they perceived the spiritual situation, they gave the gifts that, in the providence of God, enabled Joseph to take Christ to Egypt and thus to save his life. So, " while the direct meaning of the star of Bethlehem may never become known, the indirect meaning is clear and important. It states that science can guide men to God and to Christ." [14]

Thus Sikorsky's thought becomes a way of relating science and religion. It is motivated by a basic religious outlook, a spiritual interpretation of the nature of religious reality, and a somewhat mystical mode of apprehending it. Sikorsky uses the Bible as his religious guide. He is not concerned to reconcile the Bible to science in any direct way, but rather finds in the Bible a clue to the reality of quite another realm than that with which science deals. This realm is mystically known, and science can apprehend it only when in scientists themselves the element of mysticism and awe is added to the routine attitude of the scientific mind.

Many of the scientists we have met would have difficulty accepting Sikorsky's resolution of science with faith, even as Sikorsky would have difficulty with their outlook. Yet they all seek a way of relating science to religion, even if by the negative way of denying one or the other side. They all seek a meaning beyond their science, either by extending it or by looking for another discipline and authority.

What shall we say about the situation of being a scientist as it affects one's religious thought? And what shall we say about the situation of being a religious believer as it affects one's scientific endeavors? And what shall we say about interrelatedness of science and religion as light is shed upon it by the biographies and philosophies so briefly sketched above? We cannot say much, to be sure, for if our inquiry has led us anywhere, it has led us everywhere; if it has indicated certain relationships at one place, it has canceled them at another; if it has shown us certain paths of thought in one group, it has shown the opposite somewhere else. To deal with these questions we shift from story to brief concluding commentary. Brief, that it may not appear to speak the final judgment; commentary, that it may enter a wedge of inquiry — perhaps among the very scientists themselves and certainly among their philosopher friends — as to the meaning and significance of religious speculation among men of a scientific calling.

CONCLUSIONS

" So far . . . as my observation goes, scientists do not differ as a class from other educated people in their attitude toward the problems of religion. This indicates, I think, not that the growth of science has not influenced religious thought, but rather that its influences are recognized in much the same way by religious leaders and by thoughtful people generally as by scientists themselves." [1] — Robert Andrews Millikan.

SCIENTISTS hold no religious view uniquely their own. Among them one finds the same range of religious philosophies that appears among the populace as a whole. There are scientists who are scornful of traditional religion, and those who accept a traditional religious authority with complete devotion; there are those who are attracted to the cosmological and speculative elements in religion, and others, to the humanitarian and humane elements; there are those with a confident rationalism, and others confessing a vague mystical awareness of what to them is deeper reality.

The lack of pattern is obvious. Cosmic impersonalism and Christian theism are both argued from the order in the world. Evolution is at one place regarded as a proof of God's existence, at another held to be completely irreconcilable with religious theism. The Heisenberg principle is at one place used as proof for human freedom, and at another denied as having any metaphysical implications. Technology, with its benefit for mankind, is hailed by some as a boon and cursed

by others as the root of a materialism that heads for doom.
Certainly an Anthony Standen will find himself at odds with
a Philipp Frank, and a Kelly, with the religious outlook of a
Poteat.

On what shaky ground are those pulpit preachers who suppose that to quote a scientist proves religious truth! That
such and such a scientist makes a given statement about religion is no clear vindication of it. Quite likely an equally
competent scientist considers the matter in a way that contradicts the first. This is, to be sure, a specialized aspect of
a larger truth. Religious ideas are not vindicated simply by
citing the prestige of those who hold them. The prestige may
sometimes help to assess the intrinsic claim of the idea, but
of itself it solves no problems. It proves nothing to point out
in the pulpit, as some preachers do, that God exists because a
famous scientist says so. This practice piles positive error on
top of existing confusion.

Likewise wrong are those who hold that a "scientific
spirit" implies denial of all devotion to religious creeds. Certainly the scientists themselves, for all the open-mindedness
they may have for the study of the natural world, are not unconcerned about the ultimate matters of religion. Sound scientific competence is not necessarily undercut by deep religious devotion. There should have long since been an end
to the nonsense, coming on one hand from obscurantists and
on the other from cocksure atheists, that being a scientist
precludes one from being a Christian.

The many-sided pattern of the scientists' thought can also
have more positive implications. The overwhelming number
of the credos suggests that science and religion are two categories. If this were not so, the scientists would have been
able to agree better than they have regarding the nature of
religious truth. If the situation of being a scientist carried
with it any conclusive or necessary religious implications,

then we should expect of scientists a consistent religious attitude. A general agreement regarding scientific matters contrasted with basic disagreements regarding religious matters proves that there is no clear tie between them.

A dualism between science and religion is implicit in the contention of the positivist. He believes, before he starts, that science, when carefully understood and followed, will not lead him to knowledge of a religious nature. He feels, and the variegated pattern we find in our exposition would lend him a provisional measure of support, that religious matters are personal matters and reflect opinion and individual presupposition rather than a basic reference to universal reality. The disagreement so clearly seen throughout the material of this study is derived from the fact that religion has no obvious empirical rootage.

Such agreement as comes in religion comes from outside man's own search. Some " given-ness " must be had in religion from outside man, lest in his own search for religious value man be stalled in conflict and disagreement. The incommensurability of science and religion may not only demand this outside word but make it possible to accept it without a denial of one's scientific devotion or a lessening of one's scientific competence.

The theological world has struggled not a little to achieve the balance through which revelation may guide religious insight without dictating in scientific matters. For many years following the Protestant scholasticism of the late Reformation, Biblical authority was conceived only in the Biblicistic sense; those whose sound intellect demanded freedom for scientific truth rejected both the Biblicism and the true and valid Biblical insights that went with it. Religion assumed the thought patterns of the secular philosophies of the time. How apparent this is in those philosophies which, supposing themselves to be based on science, merely echo the philosophical assumptions of the Renaissance!

In modern Biblical theology, however, the dialectical method, by which the Bible's religious dimensions may be appreciated without reinterpretation to conform to secular idealism, has come into its own. It sees in the Bible God's activity, his redeeming work toward man, and still knows that the details of the message are time-bound and colored by the limited and dated knowledge of each Biblical writer. The Bible has regained its uniqueness as an authoritative religious message without an attendant and confusing attempt to regard every jot and tittle of its content as verbally inspired.

To suggest the necessity of two areas of concern and two types of knowledge is perhaps to run the risk of a new dualism. How can religious authority be made crucial to religion, and scientific authority crucial to science, without compartmentalism? The answer is a dialectical one; not the obscurantism of Kelly and Stine, but the constantly searching balance of Lane and Poteat should be our prototype. The line between science and religion cannot be eradicated. No satisfactory religious system can be based on the data of science. When religious authority is excluded, we land in chaos, and theology becomes the continuous reporting of the chaos — the unsatisfactory attempt to draw metaphysical conclusions from analogy to physical laws. Neither should a religious system be allowed to override science. When scientific facts are made subservient to dogmas, then truth itself requires the destruction of religious authority. Only when competent science handles scientific matters and competent religion handles religious matters and a dialectical attempt to relate both to a total world view bridges the gulf between them does a true reconciliation between science and religion result. How few are the credos in either part of this book that really measure up to the dimensions of this standard!

To shear either religion or science from the unity of one's total life concern is dangerous activity. Dr. Compton's words noted at the very end of the Introduction are everlastingly important. Religion must not develop in isolation from the thought currents of its time, and scientists should speak their minds on the subject of religious faith. Scientists on the other hand must not speculate without the contributions of those who make speculation and religious understanding their chief concern. In this way an interplay will guard against mistakes; the scientists' suggestions will be corrected and assimilated by those who deal with more speculative issues; and, in the case of the specifically Christian reference, by those with a clearer perception of God's word to man. This word need not cancel the experience, but strengthen, guide, and enlighten it.

Scientific authority must be scientifically autonomous; religious authority must have religious roots. Both must be part of an adequate outlook toward life, each functioning in its own realm, yet acknowledging and accepting the role of the other in its respective sphere. The compartmentalists are not wrong in their willingness to recognize two authorities, but in their unwillingness to bring them together into a total outlook and in their failure to require rigorously that each side pursue its task in conscious recognition of the contribution of the other.

Actually every view we have studied, except enthusiasm for science and invention (a special case), consciously or subconsciously draws on two perspectives. The credos of the scientists involve ideas taken from specific schools of religious and philosophical thought. Confusion comes in proportion as the credos fail to acknowledge this fact. In the case of those credos working from science to a religious outlook, enough criticism has been introduced in the exposition to show the logical difficulty in drawing rational conclusions for religion from scientific material. Einstein's God is a God of pantheism; in his fear of anthropomorphizing, he ends with a form of humanism. The Christian theists come to the idea of a personal God, with a confusion that diminishes in proportion as they admit that they use the scientific data only to support the faith that is already in them. The nontheists generally find their science leading to a philosophical position that has no lack of adherents who give it a dogmatic tradition of its own. This position is a religious philosophy, which is as much a form of faith as any other. No pluralist can admit the validity of any exclusive religious claim; this becomes his exclusive stand. No less confusion, in fact even greater chaos, comes from those who permit a religious outlook to dictate to the area properly belonging to science. In the case of creationism, except when the issues involved are of an intrinsically scientific nature, much confusion results when Biblical authority is regarded as scientifically binding. When Biblicism gains control, scientific matters are irresponsibly tinkered with. In Sikorsky's antimaterialism such a dichotomy develops between the religious and the material sides of life that no unity can be brought about between them.

This leaves the possibility of finding a partnership between science and faith in the method of Lane and Poteat. These men both acknowledge the role of science and are loyal to its contribution to human knowledge. They also acknowledge a religious truth uniquely able to speak a decisive word of meaning to the human situation. They acknowledge the need for bringing both to bear upon our total knowledge of man's natural and ultimate environment. Here science is accepted as science, yet not turned into a new creed that makes a religion of it; religion is accepted as religion, yet not turned into a substitute for, nor an antagonist of science. Each is related to the other in such a way as to make its unique contribution to a total understanding. This method is not compartmentalism, since it acknowledges the relationship of science and faith, both in the over-all pattern and in the frank discussion of specific areas of conflict.

One final element in the credos: the element of commitment. The scientists are ready to stake their life for their faith. This is obvious in the case of men like Bush; less obvious perhaps in others. Not that they are bullheadedly determined to hold their opinions against all intrusion, but that they know the need for devoted service to the religious value to which they give an intellectual allegiance — this is the mark of the religious scientist and of every religious individual.

Existentialism is fond of pointing out the commitment involved in all thought, and we are in debt to its contribution at this point. We sometimes forget, in making generalizations about the existentialist movement, that this element of dedication does not necessarily destroy a scientific open-mindedness about scientific things. Our scientists are not poorer scientists for their willingness to commit themselves in devotion to their high ideals; they are probably better scientists for doing so, and the point at which they do is indeed a boundary mark for their deep faith.

Men are not scientific in proportion as they seek to deny this level of commitment, nor are they religious in proportion as they make of it an excuse for accepting idolatrous authority. Those of us who live in a scientific age can learn from the scientists that the measure of our open-mindedness is not running to a band wagon of nonreligion. We can also learn that the measure of our religion is not running to a blind creed.

The use of science in place of a " religious " interpretation of all existence is as false as the use of Biblical religion in place of a " scientific " explanation of natural events. Christians who live in a scientific age need have no fear that ultimate loyalty to a Biblical perspective in religion *must* destroy the possibility of acknowledging the truth in science. Freedom to pursue the truth comes within devotion to a high and noble calling. We are measured neither by an ability to believe blindly nor simply to disbelieve, but rather by our ability to relate belief to experience and experience to belief. We must have our science — root honesty in experience and high skill in the control of nature. We must also have our religious credo — basic, though not blind, devotion to a truth beyond us and a deep commitment to a cause whose purposes we are constrained to serve. It is within this framework that Christians will face a scientific age, fully acknowledging the truth in science and ultimately loyal to God in Christ.

NOTES

NOTES

NOTES TO INTRODUCTION

[1] "Science and Religion," in *Science, Philosophy and Religion*, p. 209. Conference on Science, Philosophy and Religion in Their Relation to the Democratic Way of Life, 1941.

[2] *Religion of Scientists*. The Macmillan Company, 1932.

[3] "Certain Attitudes of Present Day Physicists and Psychologists," *American Journal of Psychology*, October, 1931, pp. 664–678, and "Scientific Eminence and Church Membership," *Scientific Monthly*, December, 1931, pp. 544–549.

[4] *The Freedom of Man*, p. ix. Yale University Press, 1935.

NOTES TO CHAPTER I

[1] *The Higher Foolishness*, p. 198. The Bobbs-Merrill Company, c. 1927.

[2] *Cosmic Religion*, pp. 52 f. Covici Friede, 1931.

[3] Edward H. Cotton, ed., "The Meeting Place of Science and Religion" in *Has Science Discovered God?*, p. 97. Thomas Y. Crowell Company, c. 1931.

[4] *Cosmic Religion*, p. 102.

[5] *Out of My Later Years*, p. 30. Philosophical Library, c. 1950.

[6] Cotton, *op. cit.*, p. 97.

[7] Philipp G. Frank, "Einstein, Mach, and Logical Positivism," in Paul Arthur Schilpp, *Albert Einstein, Philosopher-Scientist*, p. 284. The Library of Living Philosophers, Inc., 1949.

[8] *Cosmic Religion*, p. 48.

[9] Cotton, *op. cit.*, p. 101.

[10] *Out of My Later Years*, p. 9.

[11] *Ibid.*, pp. 28 f.

[12] *Ibid.*, p. 12.

[13] *Ibid.*, p. 114.

[14] *Ibid.*, p. 10.

[15] *The Relation of Evolution to Religion*, pp. 10 f. American Unitarian Association, 1926.

[16] *The Higher Foolishness*, p. 197.

[17] *The Relation of Evolution to Religion*, p. 10.

[18] *Standeth God Within the Shadow*, pp. 21 f. Thomas Y. Crowell Company, c. 1901.

[19] Hermann Weyl, *The Open World*, pp. 28 f. Yale University Press, 1932.

[20] *The God of Science*. The Arya Company, 1928.

[21] *Ibid.*, p. 122.
[22] *Ibid.*, p. 290.
[23] *Ibid.*, p. 291. Italics and capitals his, in this and all following quotations.
[24] *Ibid.*, p. 194.

[25] *Ibid.*, p. 257.
[26] *Ibid.*, p. 102.
[27] *Ibid.*, p. 169.
[28] *Ibid.*, p. 170.
[29] *Ibid.*, p. 145.
[30] *Ibid.*, p. 206.

NOTES TO CHAPTER II

[1] *The Religion of a Scientist,* a pamphlet, p. 15. Jewish Theological Seminary of America, 1938.

[2] *The Freedom of Man,* p. 81. Yale University Press, 1935.

[3] *Ibid.,* p. 73. Cf. *The Human Meaning of Science,* p. 62. The University of North Carolina Press, 1940.

[4] *The Religion of a Scientist,* p. 10.

[5] *Ibid.,* p. 9.

[6] *Ibid.,* p. 15. Reprinted by permission of the publishers, J. B. Lippincott Company, from "Watchers in the Sky," from *Collected Poems in One Volume,* by Alfred Noyes. Copyright, 1922, 1947, by Alfred Noyes.

[7] *The Freedom of Man,* p. 23.

[8] *The Religion of a Scientist,* p. 13. Cf. *The Freedom of Man,* p. 75.

[9] *The Religion of a Scientist,* p. 13. Cf. *The Freedom of Man,* p. 76.

[10] *The Freedom of Man,* pp. 120 f.

[11] *Ibid.,* p. 59.

[12] *Ibid.,* pp. 113 f.

[13] *Ibid.,* p. 114.

[14] *Ibid.,* p. 115.

[15] *The Human Meaning of Science,* p. 18.

[16] *Ibid.,* p. 28.

[17] *Ibid.,* p. 26.

[18] "Science Improving American Civilization," an address over the Columbia Broadcasting System, August 17, 1934. The Crusaders, Inc.

[19] "Modern Physical Science — Its Relation to Religion," in Edward H. Cotton, ed., *Has Science Discovered God?,* p. 57.

[20] *Ibid.,* p. 74.

[21] *Ibid.,* p. 70.

[22] *Science Is a Sacred Cow,* pp. 198 f. E. P. Dutton & Co., Inc., 1950.

[23] *Ibid.,* p. 200.

[24] "Science Without God," in *The Sign,* XXX, No. 2 (September, 1950), p. 49.

[25] *Ibid.,* p. 51.

[26] *Ibid.,* p. 50.

[27] *Ibid.*

[28] *Science Is a Sacred Cow,* pp. 157 f.

[29] *Ibid.,* p. 156.

[30] *Ibid.,* p. 200.

[31] *Tributes to William North Rice.* Wesleyan University Club, January 29, 1915.

[32] *Christian Faith in an Age of Science,* p. 338. A. G. Armstrong and Son, 1903.

[33] *Ibid.,* pp. 337 f.

[34] *Science and Religion,* p. 52. The Abingdon Press, c. 1925.

[35] *Ibid.*

[36] *Christian Faith in an Age of Science,* p. 302.
[37] *Ibid.,* p. 337.
[38] *Ibid.,* p. 319.
[39] *Ibid.,* p. 279.
[40] *Ibid.,* p. 284.
[41] *Science and Religion,* p. 24.

NOTES TO CHAPTER III

[1] *Evolution in Science and Religion,* pp. 13 f. Yale University Press, 1935.

[2] Reprinted in R. A. Millikan, *Science and Life,* pp. 86–90. The Pilgrim Press, 1924.

The scientists who signed were: C. D. Walcott, head, Smithsonian Institution, and president, American Association for the Advancement of Science; H. F. Osborn, president, American Museum of Natural History; E. G. Conklin, head, Department of Zoology, Princeton University; J. R. Angell, psychologist, president of Yale University; J. M. Coulter, head, Department of Botany, University of Chicago; Michael J. Pupin, physicist and engineer, professor of electromechanics, Columbia University; W. J. Mayo, surgeon, Mayo Foundation; G. D. Birkhoff, head, Department of Mathematics, Harvard University; A. A. Noyes, chemist, and director, Gates Chemical Laboratory, California Institute of Technology; W. W. Campbell, astronomer, Lick Observatory; J. J. Carthy, engineering vice-president in charge of research, American Telephone and Telegraph Company; R. A. Millikan, physicist, director of Norman Bridge Laboratory of Physics, Pasadena, California; W. H. Welsh, pathologist, Johns Hopkins Institute; J.

C. Merriam, paleontologist, president, Carnegie Institute; G. Dunn, engineer, chairman, National Research Council.

[3] *Evolution and Religion in Education.* Charles Scribner's Sons, 1926.

[4] *Evolution and Religion in Education,* p. 184.

[5] *Ibid.,* p. 7.

[6] " Evolution and Religion " in William M. Goldsmith, *Evolution or Christianity,* p. 133. The Anderson Press, 1924.

[7] *Ibid.*

[8] *Evolution in Science and Religion,* p. 41.

[9] *Science and Life,* p. 59.

[10] *Time, Matter, and Values,* p. 84. The University of North Carolina Press, 1932.

[11] *Science and Life,* pp. 2 f.

[12] *Evolution in Science and Religion,* p. 65.

[13] *Ibid.,* p. 90.

[14] *Ibid.,* p. 84.

[15] *Science and Life,* p. 53.

[16] *Evolution in Science and Religion,* pp. 56 f.

[17] *Ibid.,* p. 51.

[18] *Time, Matter, and Values,* p. 96.

[19] *Ibid.,* p. 98.

[20] *Science and Life,* p. 42.

[21] *Ibid.,* p. 37.

[22] *Human Destiny.* Longmans, Green & Co., Inc., 1947.

[23] *Ibid.,* p. 87.

[24] *Ibid.,* p. 97.
[25] *Ibid.,* p. 8.
[26] *Ibid.,* p. 84.
[27] *Ibid.,* p. 87.
[28] *Ibid.,* p. 104.
[29] *Ibid.,* p. 109.
[30] *Ibid.,* p. 174.
[31] *Ibid.,* p. 229.
[32] *Ibid.,* p. 172.
[33] Address in memory of Dr. Henry M. Howe, p. 5. Delivered at Cathedral of St. John the Divine, New York, October 25, 1923.
[34] *Ibid.*
[35] *The New Reformation,* p. 268. Charles Scribner's Sons, 1927.
[36] *Ibid.,* p. 269.
[37] Address in memory of Dr. Howe, p. 6.
[38] *Ibid.,* p. 7.

NOTES TO CHAPTER IV

[1] *A Scientist's Approach to Religion,* p. vi. Selections from Carl Wallace Miller, *A Scientist's Approach to Religion,* copyright, 1947, by The Macmillan Company and used with their permission.
[2] *Ibid.,* p. v.
[3] *Science in Search of God,* p. 77. Henry Holt Co., 1928.
[4] *The Quest for Security,* Russell Lectures, 1932, Lecture No. 5, p. 1. Auburn Theological Seminary; typescript in Union Theological Seminary Library.
[5] *Ibid.,* Lecture 5, p. 1.
[6] *Science in Search of God,* p. 118.
[7] *The Quest for Security,* Lecture No. 3, p. 3.
[8] *Science in Search of God,* p. 146.
[9] *Ibid.,* p. 28.
[10] *Ibid.,* p. 141.
[11] *Ibid.,* pp. 69 f.
[12] *Ibid.,* p. 72.
[13] *Ibid.,* p. 70.
[14] *Ibid.,* pp. 129 f.
[15] *The Quest for Security,* Lecture No. 5, p. 15.
[16] *Ibid.,* Lecture No. 4, p. 13.
[17] *A Scientist's Approach to Religion.*
[18] *Ibid.,* p. 27.
[19] *Ibid.,* p. 17.
[20] *Ibid.,* p. 20.
[21] *Ibid.,* pp. 18 f.
[22] *Ibid.,* p. 14.
[23] *Ibid.,* p. 97.
[24] *Ibid.,* p. 65.
[25] *Ibid.,* p. 67.
[26] *Ibid.,* p. 64.
[27] *Ibid.,* p. 106.
[28] *Ibid.,* pp. 69 f.
[29] *Ibid.,* p. 31.
[30] *Ibid.,* pp. 30 f.
[31] *Ibid.,* p. 125.
[32] *Ibid.*
[33] *Ibid.,* p. 102.
[34] *Ibid.,* p. 104.
[35] *Ibid.,* pp. 92 f.
[36] *Ibid.,* pp. 108 f.
[37] *Ibid.,* p. 113.
[38] *Man, Real and Ideal,* pp. 192 f. Charles Scribner's Sons, 1943.
[39] " As Intelligent as Science " in W. E. Garrison, *Faith of the Free,* p. 33. Willett, Clark & Company, 1940.

NOTES TO CHAPTER V

[1] *Reflections of a Physicist,* p. 318. Philosophical Library, 1950.

[2] *Ibid.,* p. 371.

[3] *Modern Arms and Free Men.* Simon and Schuster, Inc., 1949. Reprinted from *Modern Arms and Free Men* by permission of Simon and Schuster, Inc. Copyright, 1949, by The Trustees of the Vannevar Bush Trust.

[4] *Ibid.,* p. 171.

[5] *Ibid.,* p. 186.

[6] *Ibid.,* p. 188.

[7] *Ibid.,* p. 183.

[8] *Ibid.,* p. 186.

[9] *Ibid.*

[10] *Ibid.*

[11] *Reflections of a Physicist,* pp. 102 f.

[12] *Ibid.,* pp. 257 f.

[13] *Ibid.,* p. 44.

[14] *Ibid.,* p. 283.

[15] *Ibid.,* p. 337.

[16] *Ibid.,* p. 288.

[17] *Ibid.,* p. 100.

[18] *Ibid.,* p. 147.

[19] *Ibid.,* p. 99.

[20] *Between Physics and Philosophy.* Harvard University Press, 1941.

[21] *Ibid.,* pp. 112 f.

[22] *Relativity: a Richer Truth.* The Beacon Press, Inc., 1950.

[23] *Ibid.,* pp. 112 f.

[24] *Ibid.,* p. 82.

[25] *Ibid.,* pp. 130 f.

[26] *Ibid.,* p. 121.

[27] *Ibid.,* p. 94.

[28] *Ibid.,* pp. 107 f.

NOTES TO CHAPTER VI

[1] *Short Stories of Science and Invention,* p. 5. General Motors Corporation, n.d.

[2] *Ibid.,* p. 37.

[3] *Science, the Soul of Prosperity,* Address delivered at Modern Pioneers Dinner, Rochester, New York. National Association of Manufacturers, 1940.

[4] "Engineering and Social Progress," *Journal of Engineering Education,* XXX (1939), reprint.

[5] *Scientists Face the World of 1942,* p. 9. Rutgers University Press, 1942.

[6] *Ibid.,* p. 10.

[7] *Short Stories of Science and Invention,* p. 103.

[8] *Ibid.,* pp. 40 f.

[9] *Ibid.,* p. 9.

[10] *Ibid.,* p. 93.

[11] *Ibid.,* p. 5.

NOTES TO CHAPTER VII

[1] *Evolution, Creation and Science,* p. 63. (2d ed.) Review & Herald Publishing Association, c. 1944, 1947.

[2] E. Ralph Hooper, *Does Science Support Evolution?,* p. 12. Defender Publishers, c. 1931. Reprinted by permission. Evangelical Publishers, Toronto 1, Canada.

3 *Ibid.*, p. 21.
4 *Ibid.*, adapted and rearranged from pp. 104, 105.
5 Frank Lewis Marsh, *Evolution, Creation and Science*, p. 10.
6 *Ibid.*, p. 362.
7 *Ibid.*, p. 18.
8 *Ibid.*, p. 33.
9 *Ibid.*, p. 309.
10 *Ibid.*, p. 27.
11 *Ibid.*, p. 63.
12 *Ibid.*, p. 327.
13 *Ibid.*, p. 162.

14 *Ibid.*, p. 370.
15 *Ibid.*
16 Louis Trenchard More, *The Dogma of Evolution* (Vanuxem Lectures). Princeton University Press, 1925.
17 *Ibid.*, pp. 8 f.
18 *Ibid.*, p. 303.
19 *Ibid.*, p. 319.
20 *Ibid.*, p. 352.
21 *Ibid.*, p. 354.
22 *Ibid.*, pp. 334 f.
23 *Ibid.*, p. 364.

NOTES TO CHAPTER VIII

1 Article I.
2 Constitution of the ASA, Article II.
3 *Modern Science and Christian Faith*. Van Kampen Press, c. 1948, 1950.
4 *Astronomy*, Peter W. Stoner, chairman, Department of Mathematics and Astronomy, Pasadena City College; *Geology*, Edwin K. Gedney, professor with previous training in science, Gordon College of Theology; *Biology*, William J. Tinkle, formerly professor and head of the Department of Biology, Taylor University, Upland, Indiana, and Walter E. Lammerts, horticultural consultant to Manchester Boddy, Rancho del Descanso, La Canada, California; *Anthropology*, William A. Smalley, missionary among the Stieng tribespeople of southern French Indo-China, and Marie Fetzer, instructor in anthropology at Wheaton College; *Archaeology*, Allan A. MacRae, president of Faith Theological Seminary and professor of Old Testament; *Medical Science*, William R. Vis, practicing physician, Grand Rapids; *Chemistry*, R. Laird Harris, professor of Biblical exegesis with previous training in science, Faith Theological Seminary; *Psychology*, a Christian psychiatrist, remaining anonymous; and *Physics*, Frank Allen, retired head, Department of Physics, University of Manitoba.
5 *Modern Science and Christian Faith*, p. vii.
6 *Ibid.*, p. 259.
7 *Ibid.*, p. 104.
8 *Ibid.*, p. 136.

NOTES TO CHAPTER IX

1 *Out of Doubt Into Faith*, a pamphlet without pagination. American Tract Society, n.d.
2 *A Scientific Man and the Bible*. About 1925. Subsequently published by Harper & Bros., New York.
3 *Out of Doubt Into Faith*.

4 *A Scientific Man and the Bible*, p. 23.

5 *Out of Doubt Into Faith.*

6 *A Scientific Man and the Bible*, p. 41.

7 *Ibid.*, p. 48.

8 *Ibid.*, p. 52.

9 *Ibid.*

10 *Ibid.*, p. 54.

11 *Ibid.*

12 *Ibid.*, p. 58.

13 *Ibid.*, pp. 65 f.

14 *Ibid.*, p. 94.

15 *A Chemist and His Bible.* Sunday School Times, 1943.

16 Ps. 139:14, K.J.V.

17 Heb. 11:3, K.J.V.

18 *A Chemist and His Bible*, p. 35.

19 *Man in the Making.* The Lutheran Literary Board, 1930.

20 *Ibid.*, p. 35.

21 *Man in the Making*, p. 40.

22 *A Chemist and His Bible*, p. 7.

23 *Ibid.*, p. 18.

NOTES TO CHAPTER X

1 *Can a Man Be a Christian Today?*, pp. 70 f. The University of North Carolina Press, 1926.

2 *Science and Belief in God.* Deseret News Press, 1924.

3 *Ibid.*, p. 215.

4 *Ibid.*, p. 179.

5 *Ibid.*, p. 79.

6 *Ibid.*, p. 62.

7 *Strength of Religion as Shown by Science*, p. 45. F. A. Davis Company, c. 1926.

8 *Ibid.*, p. 50.

9 *Ibid.*, p. 202. Italics his.

10 *Evolution and Christian Faith.* Princeton University Press, 1923.

11 *Ibid.*, p. 199. Italics his.

12 *Ibid.*, p. 198. Italics his.

13 *Ibid.*, p. 167.

14 *Ibid.*, p. 152.

15 *Ibid.*

16 *Ibid.*, p. 189.

17 *Ibid.*

18 *The New Peace.* Richard G. Badger, c. 1915.

19 *Can a Man Be a Christian Today?*

20 *Ibid.*, p. 68.

21 *Ibid.*, pp. 32 f.

22 *Ibid.*, p. 36.

23 *Ibid.*, p. 69.

24 *Ibid.*, p. 99.

25 *Ibid.*, pp. 45 f.

26 *Ibid.*, p. 62.

27 *Ibid.*, p. 65.

28 *Ibid.*, p. 27.

29 *Religious Perspectives of College Teaching in the Physical Sciences.* Pamphlet, p. 19. Edward W. Hazen Foundation, Inc., 1951.

30 "Science and Religion," an address delivered at St. John's University, Brooklyn, New York, November 19, 1939. *Vital Speeches*, Vol. VI (December 15, 1939), p. 145.

31 *Religious Perspectives of College Teaching in the Physical Sciences*, p. 26.

32 *Ibid.*, p. 16.

33 *Ibid.*, p. 17.

34 "Science and Human Affairs," *Commonweal*, Vol. XXXVIII (April 30, 1943), p. 32.

NOTES TO CHAPTER XI

1 *The Invisible Encounter,* p. 94. Charles Scribner's Sons, 1947.

2 *The Invisible Encounter.*

3 *Ibid.,* pp. 31 f.

4 *Ibid.,* p. 99.

5 *Ibid.,* p. 3.

6 *The Message of the Lord's Prayer,* p. 23. Charles Scribner's Sons, 1942.

7 *The Invisible Encounter,* pp. 58 f.

8 *Ibid.,* p. 63.

9 *The Message of the Lord's Prayer,* p. 10.

10 *The Invisible Encounter,* p. 120.

11 *The Message of the Lord's Prayer,* p. 34.

12 *Ibid.,* p. 45.

13 *The Invisible Encounter,* p. 120.

14 *The Message of the Lord's Prayer,* p. 6.

NOTES TO CONCLUSIONS

1 *Evolution in Science and Religion,* p. 5.

INDEX

INDEX